WEARABLE
CRAFTS

WEARABLE CRAFTS

creating clothing, body
adornments, and jewelry
from fabrics and fibers

BY ELYSE AND MIKE SOMMER

Crown Publishers, Inc., New York

Printed in the United States of America
Published simultaneously in Canada by General Publishing
Company Limited

Design: Deborah Daly

Library of Congress Cataloging in Publication Data

Sommer, Elyse.
  Wearable crafts.

  Bibliography: p.
  Includes index.
  1. Textile crafts. 2. Clothing and dress.
3. Jewelry making—Amateurs' manuals. I. Sommer,
Mike, joint author. II. Title.
TT699.S64 1976   746   75-40250
ISBN 0-517-52395-7
ISBN 0-517-52518-7 pbk.

Contents

Foreword and Acknowledgments

This book is a salute to all those who have applied their vision and artistry to the skills once dubbed as "just handicrafts." By having the courage to break with the use of traditional materials they have also broken down the barriers that have confined jewelry, accessories, and clothing within separate, distinct categories, each to be fashioned in their own "acceptable" materials. The creators of wearable crafts have reconfirmed the importance of function in crafts. The individuality of their work has validated the concept that a design which is hung on the body can be art. Yet, being ever inventive, these craftspeople have often managed to combine both wall art and body art by creating clothing and jewelry which can function independently as hangings or sculptures. We've tried to search out as many of these double-duty ideas as possible for those readers who love beautiful things but prefer their clothing to be of the utmost and unembellished simplicity. Many artists have created designs especially geared to this concept and we owe them and all others who contributed to this book an irreparable debt of gratitude. Our contacts with the artists who coauthored this book were joyful and rewarding experiences. Everyone we met and corresponded with was truly special: spontaneous, gifted, fun and serious and, above all, giving—ready to share their own work and ideas while eager to bring us in contact with their friends and colleagues.

In organizing the material for this book we began with the concept of having chapters devoted to types of body coverings such as hats, necklaces, waistbands, and so on. Books like this have a way of eluding preconceived plans and developing their own shape and form. Thus, while we ended up grouping ideas according to crafts materials and the skills involved in using them, there is still no tightly controlled system of classification. Many crafts skills can be used by themselves or in combination with others, and many illustrations found in one chapter might easily have fitted into another. Our choice of placement was dictated not only by the compatibility of techniques but also of ideas, for this *is* basically an idea book.

There are no specific materials you must have or techniques you must master. A collar necklace or waistcoat can be made with scraps of fabric and yarn, using patchwork and/or quilting, weaving, crocheting, knotting, netting, or a combination of methods. The addition of beads, stones, ceramics, or metals will make these essentially soft forms into soft-hard ones.

The demonstrations are simple enough for beginners to follow. Techniques used can be mastered quickly and with a minimum of equipment. Those already familiar with some of the skills illustrated will find many shortcuts and innovations. The Bibliography can serve as a directory for all who wish to go into a particular craft in depth.

If this book brings to the reader just a measure of the enjoyment that putting it together has brought us, then our purpose will have been fulfilled and our pleasure heightened.

All work unless otherwise identified by Elyse Sommer.
All photographs unless otherwise identified by Mike Sommer.

Elyse and Mike Sommer
Woodmere, Long Island,
New York

WEARABLE
CRAFTS

THE DEVELOPMENT OF BODY ADORNMENTS AND SOFT JEWELRY

The terms soft jewelry, body craft, and portable and wearable art are fairly recent additions to the history of body adornment, which dates back to the very beginning of mankind.

Although clothing and jewelry have always been closely allied, society's need to categorize and define has set up certain artificial barriers which have identified jewelry with metals and stones, dress with utilitarian body coverings, and adornments with anything added to dress beyond that considered necessary. Thus, those interested in jewelry making have for centuries thought of metals and stones as their primary media. Even the popularization of costume jewelry in the 1930s did not alter jewelry's essential "hardness," since costume jewelry was made in most instances with materials designed to resemble precious stones and metals. Fabrics wrought with hooks and needles and embellished with stitchery were still classified as dress adornments.

The same duality which allies clothing and jewelry as complementary fashions, while separating them in terms of the materials considered "proper" for their creation, also affects the motivation behind people's choice of what to wear. On the one hand, there is a basic instinct for beauty and comfort; on the other, a need to present a certain image or face to the world around us.

During many periods of history, the image presented through one's manner of personal dress was prescribed by rigid customs, and often by laws, such as those forbidding anyone without a certain rank or income to wear precious stones, or clothing wrought with metallic threads. Even as societies became more democratic, traditional mores continued to dictate: Overalls and work shirts identified the laborer; precious and semiprecious stones and metals were worn not just for beauty but for status, and clothing that was not new or in the latest style was associated with low or no status.

The last decade or so truly marks a new era in body adornment. Mass production and affluence made it possible for everybody to be in fashion. More people owned more things than ever before, but after a while everything tended to look alike. The young, especially, began to yearn more for individuality than for correctness or stylishness. They began to reexamine their life-styles and possessions and those of their ancestors.

They began to think that perhaps machine-made, or at least factory machine-made, was not better than handmade. Maybe the skills of our forebears could be relearned, this time not just out of necessity but to fill an artistic need. The availability of many beautiful fabrics, a rich palette of fibers, and easy-to-use, waterproof paint products made this idea appealing and viable for novices and experienced artists alike. Home sewing machines with the facility to produce decorative as well as utilitarian stitches, and the concept of using ready-made clothing as canvases for embellishments, offered the best of both worlds to those attracted to the concept of handcrafted wearables but unwilling or unable to devote a great deal of time to creative effort.

Probably the most popular canvases for this new breed of artists have been the T-shirt and blue denim clothes, both of which had humble origins.

The T-shirt was once a type of French underwear. During World War I, American doughboys adopted it as a comfortable alternative to the wool union suit. The basic round neck and placket front, shaped like the letter T, accounted for the name. The T-shirt emerged as a "Tee" shirt during the 1940s, when it became a popular golf fashion.

Donata Stern has literally taken some of her favorite paintings off the wall. The details of her framed canvases are somewhat simplified . . .

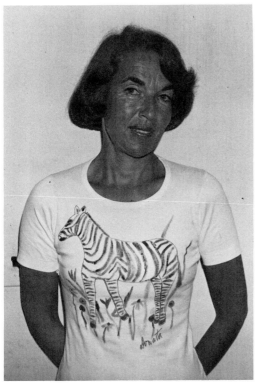

. . . when translated onto a classic T-shirt, modeled here by the artist. (See color section.)

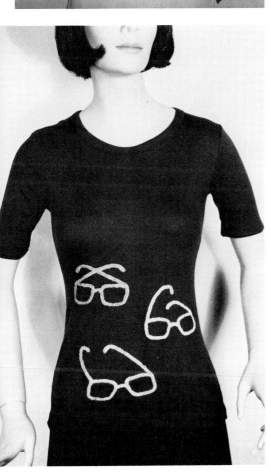

T-shirts take very well to embroidery, which can be intricate and elaborate like this shirt from India . . .

. . . or simple and humorous like this one.

Denim pants and jackets are probably the most universally de-
mocratizing fashion of the twentieth century. They have enjoyed a
steady, if initially unfashionable, success as work clothes since the
middle of the nineteenth century, when a young immigrant named
Levi Strauss set up in the trouser business to make his fortune
serving the miners of the West. Since World War II, denim pants
have become a favorite with first the young, then eventually with
practically anyone, anywhere. The older and more worn the pants,
the better. It was this attachment to the worn-in that led to the
decorative recycling of the worn-out.

In 1972 the Levi Strauss Company sponsored a denim art con-
test which drew more than two thousand entries from the United
States, Canada, and the Bahamas. The winning entries became
part of a traveling exhibit making stops at various museums. This
has stimulated still further interest in this uniquely contemporary
kind of art.

This portrait of actor Ed Den-
nehy was appliquéd in velvet,
satins, gold, brocade, and
gold buttons by Margaret Cusack as a gift for the actor by
producer Bob Demchuk.
Photo courtesy artist.

Edward Goss in a pair of pants
lovingly patched by Elaine
Goss.

Dee Webber's denim suit is an assemblage of old sewing notions.

Rear view of Dee Webber's denim suit. (See page 77 for an embroidered denim jacket.)

Once artists and hobbyists became caught up in the possibilities inherent in clothing decoration with a variety of fiber and fabric techniques, the embellishments grew more and more elaborate. This led to an interest in creating clothing which was art as well as a body covering and in designing embellishments or soft jewelry which could be worn independently rather than attached to clothing. The division between clothing and jewelry became more and more blurred. A fabric neckpiece could be a collar or a necklace. A necklace made with soft materials had none of the limitations of size and weight imposed by traditional metals, so that it could grow into a vest or cape. In short, clothing could be jewelry; jewelry, clothing.

A modern jeweler is as likely to own a sewing machine as a jeweler's saw, and to refer to historic examples of costume as well as jewelry as inspiration for methods, materials, and designs. Painters and sculptors are in turn recognizing clothing as a way of creating art which is not confined to museum and gallery walls but can be seen and enjoyed by a much larger audience. Thus, every busy street corner is a veritable gallery of portable art; a self-judging one to be sure, since not every painted or embroidered T-shirt or handmade garment is of museum quality.

Happily, the new soft jewelers and creators of wearable art have not lost the acceptance of the art world by taking their work off museum walls and into the street, so to speak. On the contrary, the originality and diversity of fabric and fiber jewelry and adornments has been accompanied by a growing interest in wearable art on the part of curators and gallery owners. Shows partially or entirely devoted to body craft, personal adornment, wearable and/or soft art have become a regular part of the gallery scene throughout the country. The Museum of Contemporary Crafts in New York, the Portland Museum in Oregon, the Southwest Crafts Center in Texas, and the Los Angeles County Museum in California are just some of the institutions that have mounted several such shows.

The creation of jewelry and body adornments from fabrics and fibers, whether pursued as a hobby or as a serious art form, is a way of making a very personal statement. If offers an opportunity to express one's taste, talents, humor, and fantasies. Ideas for what and how to create can be found in our immediate environment or in the past.

This beautiful dress was made in Russia during the nineteenth century. Courtesy The Metropolitan Museum of Art, Gift of Miss Isabel Hapgood, 1911.

Louise Todd Cope is a contemporary textile artist inspired by the patchwork tradition, as shown in her Recycled Island Dress. Photo courtesy artist.

Early Egyptian wigs fascinate many contemporary fiber artists. This one of Princess Nany (ca. 1000 B.C.) has braids of hair set with beeswax and woven into linen string to form a cap. Courtesy The Metropolitan Museum of Art, Museum Excavations, 1928–29.

Jean Boardman Knorr's wiglike head adornment was crocheted with thick Mexican yarns.

Fiber artist Dolly Curtis made her Cleopatra's Wig of linen and jute in basketry techniques—knotted, plaited, and plied. Gold coins were added for decoration. Photo, Victor Cromwell.

Francie Allen's fascination with the shape of ancient Egyptian wigs inspired this knotted and crocheted Medicine Hat. Photo, Roger Rosenblatt.

9

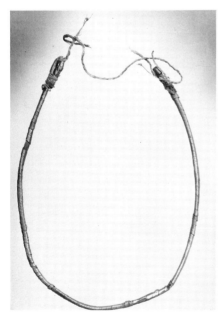

Another unusual source of inspiration for head and body coverings: natural fibers braided and wrapped right into their own hair by women of New Guinea. Photo, Musée de L'Homme.

The use of bright yarns for wrapping has made it a favorite technique with soft-jewelers like Madge Copeland.

We needed an entire chapter to describe the many contemporary uses of wrapping. This collar of bright golden straw over grass coil cords dates back to the Egyptian Eleventh Dynasty. Photo courtesy The Metropolitan Museum of Art, Museum Excavations, Rogers Fund, 1931.

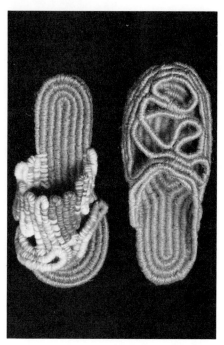

Woven papyrus sandals, Egyptian Eighteenth Dynasty. Photo courtesy The Metropolitan Museum of Art, Museum Excavations 1920–22, Rogers Fund.

Mary Lou Higgins's beige and hot-pink wrapped slippers echo the Egyptian era. Photo, Edward Higgins.

Feathers have long been part of the personal adornments of many civilizations. Examples like this breastplate from Polynesia stimulate modern feather workers to create new designs. Photo courtesy Field Museum of Natural History.

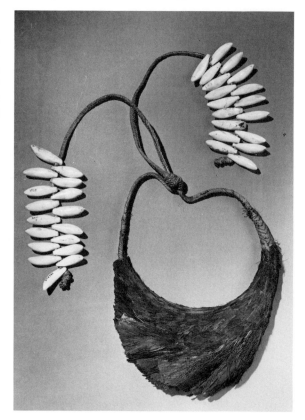

11

This breastplate, entitled Proud Bird III, is the work of Nicki Marx, whose elegant feather jewelry has won national recognition. Photo courtesy artist.

Crocheters and knotless netters as well as embroiderers will find much to admire in this unusual pre-Inca necklace embroidered in wool in point bouclé. Photo courtesy The Metropolitan Museum of Art, Gift of George D. Pratt, 1929.

This garment, designed and stitched by Dewey Lipe, is in its elegance and style reminiscent of the lavishly embroidered tunics once worn by nobles and ecclesiastics. But the three-dimensional crochet and knotless netting embellishments of course mark this as a distinctly "now" body covering. Photo courtesy artist.

Dainty aprons with French embroidery were popular workbasket projects during the nineteenth and early twentieth centuries. This sample is from an old issue of the now-defunct magazine *The Modern Priscilla*.

Reta Miller uses the old-fashioned dainty apron as an inspiration for her humorous stitched commentaries on the old traditions.

2

PAINTED AND PRINTED FABRICS

Although textile companies are offering an ever-increasing array of attractive prints, there is something irresistible about creating one's own designs on fabric. Even something as simple as lettering can be individualized by the use of color, the addition of symbols, the variation of type.

Water-based acrylic paints have been a particular boon to the fabric painter. They dry fast, allowing the artist to make changes and apply shading and details without having to wait for the initial coat of paint to dry. Textile paints and dyes further expand the fabric artist's range of available colors and effects.

The simplicity and directness of drawing with solid colors has held appeal to do-it-yourself buffs for more than half a century. Editors of *The Modern Priscilla*, a home-service magazine, often printed motifs to be applied with crayons to scarves and other wearables. And the modern-day permanent, waterproof felt-tip pens make drawing on fabric smoother and of course more diversified, thanks to the many colors being manufactured.

Most artists, regardless of what painting or printing techniques they use, prefer to work with natural fibers. These accept color pigments more readily than do synthetics. However, some coloring methods which have come into use are specifically made for synthetics, so that anything is indeed possible.

The following painting and printing presentations offer just some of the approaches and methods available. Since space has dictated using an overview approach, the focus is on simplicity.

Readers wishing to pursue any of these techniques in depth are referred to the Bibliography.

To start, here are some general rules to keep in mind when decorating fabrics:

1.   Most paints, markers, and dyes work best on natural fabrics such as cotton, linen, muslin, silk, and wool.
2.   Always wash fabrics to be painted, to remove any sizing.
3.   When working with a sewn garment, be sure to slip a plastic-covered palette board (corrugated cardboard is fine) in between the front and back portions to prevent paint from seeping through. Save for this purpose the plastic bags used by dry cleaners. Even unsewn fabric is easier to work on if pinned on top of a board. An ironing board makes a dandy base.
4.   To ensure the permanence of colors (optional for acrylic paints), the design should be heat set. This can be done by pressing the finished item with a steam iron for about five minutes, tumbling it in a drier for twenty minutes, or wrapping it in tinfoil and baking in a low oven for about five or ten minutes. An old-fashioned but still effective color-fixing formula is to dip a piece of toweling into white vinegar, press out the excess moisture, then place the damp cloth on top of the wrong side of the fabric, and finally press it with a steam iron.

Starting to Paint on Fabrics

For the experienced painter, working on fabrics is merely a matter of using a new and more absorbent background. Designs can be traced onto fabrics using dressmakers' tracing paper and

Donata Stern, an experienced painter on canvas, had little difficulty painting on T-shirts. Many of her designs come directly from . . .

. . . paintings, like this one, photographed at the Country Art Gallery in Locust Valley, New York.

chalk, then painted inside the design's outline, coloring book fashion. They can also be painted freehand. As mentioned, the quick-drying properties of acrylics make it easy to dab on a blob of color, then add fine brush details and shading without waiting for the original application to dry. Colors can be blended while they are still wet. Although these paints are permanent, some errors, such as a too heavy application of paint, can be "erased" by dabbing on some color to match the background fabric.

When working with acrylics and other types of water-based paints, the only thinner needed is water. Very little thinning is recommended, since nonrunny paints are easier to control. Everyone, of course, finds their own perfect paint consistency, favorite type and size of brush. Marilyn Green, for example, breaks the rule about using fairly thick paint by deliberately painting her charming fabric lockets with textile paint thinned to a very runny consistency, since she wants her paint to penetrate through to the underside of the locket, creating its own second design for the lid.

Marilyn Green paints the top of her soft lockets with textile paint thinned to a runny consistency . . .

. . . so that the paint penetrates to the underside, thus creating its own secondary design.

For the novice, Joanne Ashcraft, who teaches fabric painting, recommends some easy stenciling techniques as surefire confidence builders. Stenciling, which has a long history starting in China and Japan, has long been a popular textile-decorating technique. It is a process of cutting a design out of an overlay

Stencil designs with illustrations for use on handbags, from *Ladies' World,* 1890.

material and brushing paint through the open portions. The stencil can also be used in reverse by spatter painting around the edges of an outline design or template, thus creating a negative design. In the photographs illustrating Joanne Ashcraft's designs and methods, her daughter Joanne demonstrates and models them.

A large flower design has been cut out of a paper stencil pinned to a pair of canvas boots, with acrylic paint brushed through the cutout. Shading is achieved by applying paint more heavily at the edges and more and more lightly toward the center.

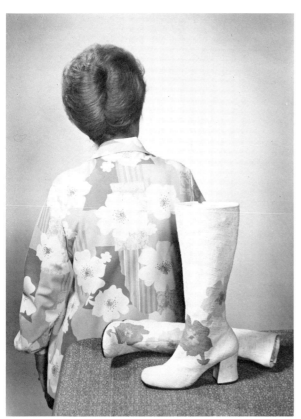

The flower stencil was cut to match the print of a store-bought shirt.

A repeated cotton-boll motif is painted with the aid of a paper stencil. Since four colors are used, four different paper stencils are cut. An ironing board serves as a palette base.

To relieve the flatness of stencil painting, details are added with a small brush. Permanent ink is used for the details, though paint would be all right too.

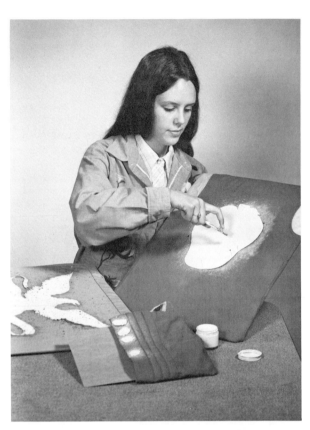

The cotton-boll design coordinates
a shirt and handbag.

For reverse stenciling, a paper outline of a strawberry is secured to the fabric with pins. Using a stiff-bristle brush and only a small amount of paint, color is spattered around the edge of the template by pulling one's finger across the bristles. The spatter should be heavier at the edge of the paper. To further simplify the painting process, the design is color coordinated with the background fabric. In this case a red shirt serves as a background for the strawberry design.

When the stencil is lifted, only the leaves and seed details need to be painted, since the portion of the red fabric formerly covered now becomes the strawberry itself. At the right front is a hat stenciled with a small strawberry template. To the left we see another stencil design, an eagle, applied onto a gray shirt with darker gray spatter, with detail lines in permanent black ink.

19

The finished eagle-stenciled shirt.

Once students have gotten used to the way fabric and paint work together, using simple paper stencils as guides, Joanne encourages them to attempt a freehand fabric painting. Trees, which have universal appeal, offer a chance to really experiment with different shapes and ways of shading. They can be painted realistically or abstractly. All kinds of details can be added with paint or ink, using as applicators found objects as well as brushes.

A tree is best begun at the base, where the brush can be applied with a broad stroke. The point is used toward the top branches for tapering effects. The dress Joanne wears features a stencil-painted design on a gingham ground.

Leaves are applied with sweeping dabs of a stiff brush. The darker leaves come first.

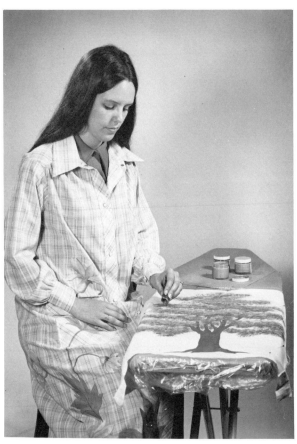

Leaf effects can be varied by alternating the brush with small sponges . . .

. . . or even bits of steel wool. After the lighter leaves have been applied, bits of the darker color can be brought back with a pad of cotton or a brush.

Small birds with names of the owner's family members have been added to the basic design for a wonderful Tree of Life shirt.

Heat Transferring Designs from Paper to Fabric

The method of heat transferring designs from paper to fabric rather than printing or painting them directly onto the fabric has become increasingly important in commercial textile printing. Patterns can be stored on paper and printed onto fabric only when needed.

For most individual artists, this type of equipment is far too expensive even to consider buying, but we feel that this is a developing technology which may well be adapted in a way that will make it a viable medium for artists and hobbyists. Several possibilities already exist.

The first is a very simple and inexpensive fabric crayon which is used on paper but can be transferred to fabric by pressing the design into the cloth with a hot iron. The color range of these crayons is not as varied as that found in permanent felt-tip pens and paints, but the simplicity of the method and the fact that these crayons, unlike other paints and dyes, are especially applicable to synthetics make them worth trying out. The design will be transferred in reverse, which must be kept in mind when using motifs with letters. It is a good idea to hold your design in front of a mirror to check how it looks in reverse. In the demonstration which follows, Susanna McVay shows how she used fabric crayons to design a handsome pinafore. (All photographs courtesy Binney & Smith, Inc.)

Susanna wanted a cityscape as an all-over design for her pinafore. She made cardboard templates to help her outline her house design onto paper.

After the design was sketched out, the houses and other details were colored in with crayon. The heavier the color is applied, the deeper the colors will be.

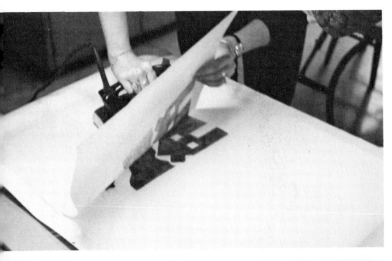

The paper design is placed on top of the fabric to be printed and then pressed with a hot iron. Fabrics must be at least 50 percent synthetic for the colors to be permanent.

Susanna measured her fabric pieces before applying the various portions of the design, but did not cut out her garment pattern until her print transfer was complete. The garment pieces could be cut out first.

The hand-printed fabric is sewn . . .

. . . and ready to wear. The paper print could be reused, but since some of the color will be lost in the heat transfer, the crayons must be reapplied.

For those who enjoy experimenting with the latest technology, there is still another type of heat transfer which can be obtained by taking a black-and-white photograph or sketch to one of the 3M Company's color-in-color centers (see Sources of Supplies) and having it made up into a matrix which can in turn be pressed onto fabric with an iron, much as fabric crayon designs. Each matrix can be used just once, so a different one must be purchased for each

Five women's neckties by Kay Shuper. The photographic images were transferred to the fabric with the color-in-color process. Five different matrices had to be made. Photo courtesy artist.

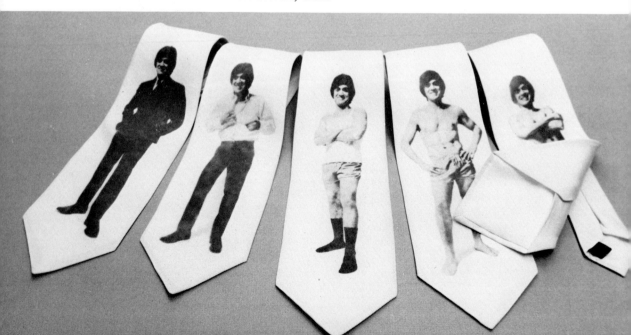

image. The machine also has a built-in color dial so that the black-and-white original can be produced in a variety of colors. Again, each color requires a different matrix.

Printing with Plastelene

Many found objects and materials can be used to hand print designs onto fabric. We discovered one of the easiest-to-use and versatile printing materials to be plastelene, the nonhardening clay available in every novelty or art store. We used acrylic paints in tubes, squeezing out about an inch of paint at a time and stirring in water until a creamy consistency was obtained. Designs are best kept simple.

When we first experimented with these printers we thought they would not hold up through the printing of a shirt. Surprisingly, the more we dipped them in paint, the stronger they became. The same basic shapes used to print the shirt as shown in the following photographs were also used to print the lining of the jacket on page 136 and several gift scarves. The forms remained intact and usable even then. They could be washed off, returned to their unformed shape, and used to make other designs.

The one precaution for keeping your fabric clean and producing a good print is to keep several rags at hand at all times. Fingers should be wiped between dipping and printing, and printers pressed down with a cloth to prevent any possibility of smudging.

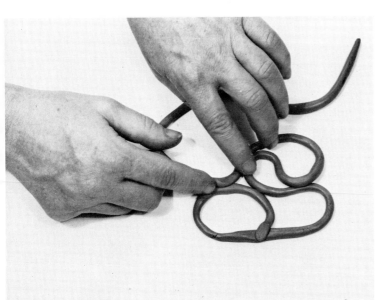

Since this type of clay often constitutes a child's first experience with a sculpting material, we decided to make one of our designs from the kind of rope most youngsters like to roll out. The clay rope was worked into a free-form pretzel shape. Areas to be attached should be firmly pressed together and the lines smoothed out before starting to print.

The printer is dipped into a pan into which acrylic paint has been mixed with water to a creamy consistency. The second printer, a solid stick figure, is at hand.

A brush is used to smooth any drippy areas and cover those which have not absorbed the paint. Since plastelene has such a smooth surface, this dip–brush–print procedure is best.

Wipe excess paint from your fingers and press the printer onto the fabric, using a clean rag to prevent smudging the material.

The printer can be lifted almost instantly. The slight unevenness of the print is due to the somewhat paint resistant surface of the clay. If the paint mixture were thicker, a more even print would result, but we like this faint resemblance to a batik crackle.

The creative advantage of this type of printing is that even if the same basic design is repeated from one item to another, the placement of each print is bound to be different. The background material and colors used offer further variations on repeated designs.

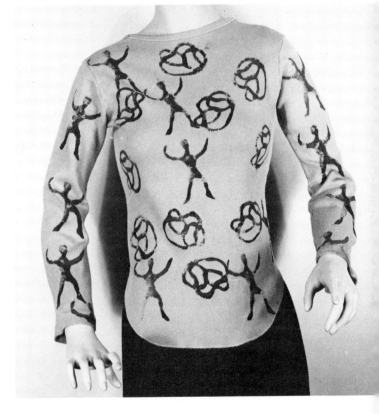

Other Quick and Easy Hand-Printing Ideas

All kinds of found objects can be enlisted to experiment with fabric designs: corks, old type blocks sold at flea markets and antique shows, buttons, keys, and so forth. Potatoes, carrots, and cork can be carved out with a kitchen or X-acto knife to make raised design printers.

Sheets of foam rubber or thin foam dish cloths sold at most supermarkets can be used much like plastelene, either as solid shapes or with relief areas cut out of the outline shapes. The foam material is more absorbent than the plastelene, and you may want to combine the two for different effects.

Printing with a Silk Screen

Hand prints are usually fairly small. When working with a large design and/or repeats, the silk-screen method has much to recommend it. Actually, silk-screening is a mechanized form of stenciling. A stencil design is applied to a piece of porous cloth, usually silk; thus the name, silk screen. The screen is stretched onto a wooden frame which is placed over the fabric to be printed, and inked. The design is then transferred from frame to fabric. If the silk is cleaned after each use it will last for a long time. Water-based inks are easier and cheaper to clean than oil-based ones.

In the following demonstration, Joellen Sommer used a 10-by-18-inch silk screen which was bought preassembled. White T-shirts were tie dyed with a circle design achieved by tying rubber bands around portions of the shirt in tight circles. The shirts were dyed with household dyes which were color set by pressing the finished shirt with a cloth dipped in vinegar. The block letters and symbol were cut out of white paper. The message being printed, by the way, is a humorous takeoff on the more obvious political symbolism, created by a group of Hewlett, Long Island, high school students who had spent much of their senior year in the student activities room and now wanted a memory shirt.

The stencil is placed onto the screen base.

The screen is inked with a squeegee to adhere the design to the top of the screen. After this initial step, the shirt to be printed (carefully folded over a thick cardboard, with sleeves to the back) is placed under the screen, which is then inked again.

When the screen is lifted, the first print is complete. The screen must be reinked for every other shirt printed. One paper stencil will last for about fifteen prints. For a larger number of prints a lacquer stencil would be preferable.

The Student Activist shirt and another shirt in a simple block lettering design.

Sheila Klein wanted an enormous shoulder bag which would be like an extension of herself while traveling. She stenciled separate pieces of her design onto heavy duck cloth which was later assembled. Some of her animal-loving friends suggested the addition of holes, which gave the bag a double life as a body bag and portable pet shelter.

John Pitts uses silk screening to foster communication for the deaf. Photo courtesy artist.

Batik

A sort of mystical aura surrounding batik work has often frightened off the untrained and unskilled. The method, which originated with the Javanese, involves working colors into fabrics by means of dipping them into dye. Before each dip, areas not to receive colors are brushed with melted wax which acts as a resist to the dye. The dyeing is thus planned in reverse, with a separate dye bath for each color. Crafts experts have for years worked at simplifying the traditional methods.

With the advent of colored waxes, batiking can be as easy as regular painting. Each color of melted wax can be applied directly onto the fabric. The entire design with all its colors can be developed at once, without overdyes. If the background is dyed, this will be the only dye bath, since the colors in the design are all wax and thus will resist the dye. Anyone wishing to use this one-step method is advised to look for colored waxes which are colorfast (see Sources of Supplies). There are alternative methods and many easy-to-use dyes being explored by artists and craftsmen. For those working in the area of body adornments, batik can be a source of much discovery and design.

Batik with Brushed-on Natural Dyes

Susanna Kuo had her initial experience with batik during two years of living in Japan, where batik is called *roketsuzome,* or ''wax dyeing.'' Susanna does not dip her batiks, nor does she use a tjanting tool. She applies her dyes with a Japanese waxing brush similar to those used for sumi painting and calligraphy. This conserves dyes and allows the artist to create shading and other effects which cannot be achieved by dipping. The dye used is a Swiss photosensitive or vat dye called Indigosol similar to Inko dyes. The color develops when the dye is exposed to ultraviolet light.

The fabric to be batiked is tacked to a frame. The original paper design pattern is placed underneath to serve as a guide for waxing. If the fabric is not sheer enough for the pattern to show through, a light table can be placed beneath the pattern and batik frame. (Light tables are also valuable tracing aids for all types of needlework and stitchery.) They can be constructed quite easily by placing two fluorescent lights inside a simple box frame with a cut-to-fit piece of smoky Plexiglas resting on the frame.

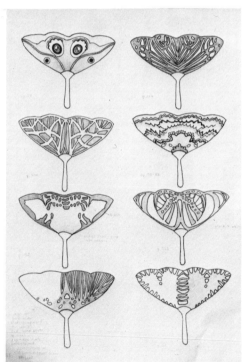

Preliminary sketches for fans.

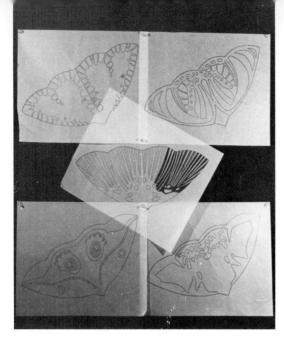

Patterns to be used as guides for waxing.

Stage one in the wax dyeing, in which the white areas have been waxed. The black lines are the pattern underneath the fabric.

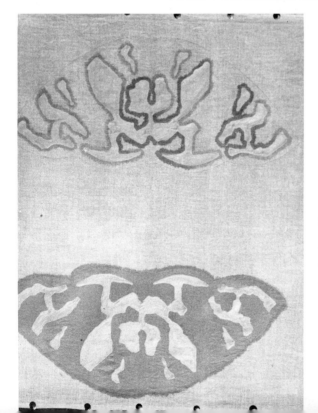

Stage two, with one side of the unwaxed area brush-dyed yellow. On the other side, only the margin around the waxed area has been brush dyed.

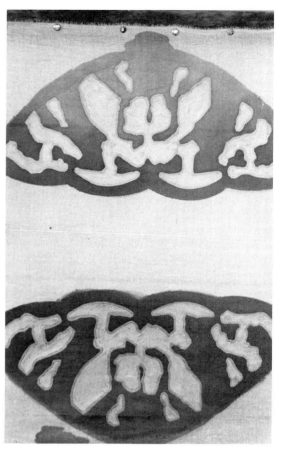

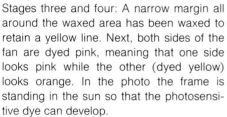

Stages three and four: A narrow margin all around the waxed area has been waxed to retain a yellow line. Next, both sides of the fan are dyed pink, meaning that one side looks pink while the other (dyed yellow) looks orange. In the photo the frame is standing in the sun so that the photosensitive dye can develop.

Stage five: Brown dye has been applied to the top (wide) margin of the fan and gradually diluted downward so that the color changes from brown to rose on one side and from brown to orange on the other. The use of a brush instead of dipping makes these fine gradations much more controllable.

A finished fan.

Here we see the artist, Susanna Kuo, at work in her studio on another fan.

Underside or inside view of Susanna Kuo's Fin Cap.

A delicate headpiece batiked in the manner just illustrated.

Preliminary sketches for the Fin Cap. The right-hand version was the one finally used.

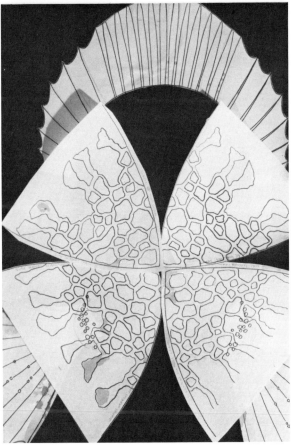

Fin Cap pattern pieces to be used as waxing guides.

Mixed-Media Batik

Susanna Kuo's sister, Ginny Adelsheim, is a potter. The two artists collaborated successfully on a neckpiece inspired by ancient Egyptian neck pectorals. Trying to match the colors in clay and dye proved an interesting experiment. Ginny found that the best way to achieve the soft colors of batik was to work oxides into a low-fired soft clay. A clear top glaze is the only one used. Susanna applied her vegetable dyes to blue green silk and rayon which had been padded and quilted. Two snaps and a broad hook and eye serve as a clasp.

Sketches for neck pectoral.

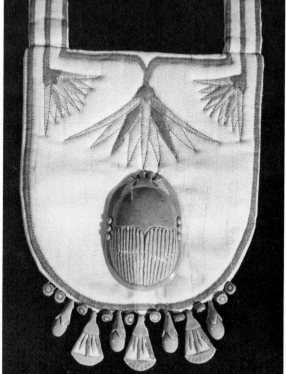

Batik and ceramic neck pectoral by Susanna Kuo and Ginny Adelsheim.

Batiking on a Miniature Scale

Just a touch of batik can add the right and distinctive focal point for a piece of soft jewelry. Marilyn Green combines many stitchery and assemblage elements in her jewelry, often including small areas of batik. She uses toothpicks and any handy pointed tool to apply wax and color to her batik designs.

Quilted neckpiece with the leaf area batiked.

Nancy Welch likes the velvety feel of wax on Pellon, a fabric normally reserved for linings. However, not only does Pellon offer an interesting background for directly applied miniature batik design but, like felt, it can be sewn without having to tuck in edges. Nancy painted the eyes of her necklace with Versatex, then waxed and later ironed out the wax.

Instant batik on Pellon decorates a necklace by Nancy Welch, aptly entitled Here's Lookin' at Ya.

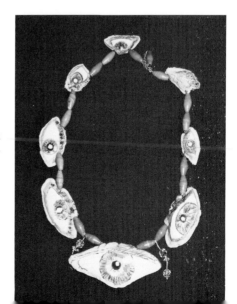

Traditional Batiking:
Painted, Waxed, Dipped

Shirley Venit Anger's batiked caftans are indeed wearable art. Her designs show a true mastery of all the traditional skills and all the possibilities inherent therein.

A sleeveless caftan-wall hanging entitled Musicians, by Shirley Venit Anger. Photo, Herman Beck.

Another batik on silk caftan by Shirley Venit Anger.

Lonely People, a caftan-wall hanging by Shirley Venit Anger. Photo, Herman Beck.

3

APPLIQUÉD, PATCHED, AND QUILTED FABRICS

Appliqué, patchwork, and quilting methods are to one who sews what collage, decoupage, and montage are to the painter. Commercially printed fabrics cut, reshaped, and sewn to conform to the artist's vision become totally new statements. And the addition of stuffing adds a sculptural dimension to sewn work.

Appliqués can be created by sketching an outline for an original design and then coloring in the appropriate fabrics. Margaret Cusack, for example, often uses methods she learned while studying graphic design. To make a large appliqué painting to ornament clothing she draws her design on paper, sharpening her outlines with felt-tip pens. Then she places her drawing on top of a light box and her fabric over the drawing. (*See* page 31 for instructions on making a light box.) The light will project the design through the fabric so that is can be transferred with pencils, felt-tip pens, or tailors' chalk, depending upon the fabric. When Margaret has her basic outline worked onto the fabric background, she selects and cuts other materials to fill in or complete her "painting." The final step is to stitch everything into place, which she does all by machine.

High Fashion Lady by Margaret Cusack. Satins and cut velvet are appliquéd on pale blue denim. Photo, Gary Stein.

Robbie Fanning appliquéd this coat for her field trips into California salt marshes with schoolchildren. The bottom of the coat is in three shades of blue to symbolize the tide. Photo courtesy artist.

Detail of appliquéd egret.

Some appliqués begin as nonwearable forms. For instance, this design started as an appliqué pillow by Dolly Curtis, who later decided she'd enjoy her work a lot more as part of a jacket.

Creating with Preprinted Designs: Ideas for the Fabric Decoupeur

Since selection is very much a creative process, you don't have to work out your own design patterns to be a creative appliquér. Instead, many prints can be redefined as appliqués. Fabric prints are cut out like paper for decoupage, but instead of being glued and varnished to a background they are stitched in place.

When cutting out representational print outlines, it's a good idea to spray the fabric with ironing starch, which will help to stiffen it for easy cutting. If machine zigzag stitching is used, the cutting can be done right along the edge of the design outline. For hand stitching an extra border must be cut, notched, and tucked under to prevent fraying.

Appliqué-Decoupage Vest

A cotton print of Aubrey Beardsley designs triggered the idea of recycling an old fake-fur jacket into an evening vest. The jacket was cut apart to remove the zipper closing and sleeves, and to facilitate handling of the appliqué work. The print had to be cut and redesigned in proportion to the vest. Black felt was used to reshape the voluminous bottoms of some of the costume skirts and to provide a sharper contrast against the white material.

◀

A print cut and pinned to one of the front panels of the vest. Notice the felt, added to redefine the proportions of the skirt.

The fullest print was used for the back. Cutting and notching around facial features can be a bit tricky, but if crisp scissors are used and lots of notches are cut, the tucking under can be accomplished without losing the more delicate details.

The front of the vest.

Appliqué-Decoupage Necklace

Often the shapes and forms which comprise an overall pattern can be isolated and appliquéd to a solid background for a completely new fabric look.

A busy pattern like this provides good practice for seeking out shapes within a pattern to create a new design.

Here is the basic necklace and the design used as a decorative appliqué. One of the print figures was used as a focal point, and some of the border material was cut and reshaped. Note how some of the background print has been cut to make a little pedestal to balance the central design. The prints were cut without seam allowance, since machine zigzag stitching will be used, eliminating the need to tuck raw edges under.

The finished necklace with pearl buttons used as additional surface accents and also to complete the closing for the braided felt loops.

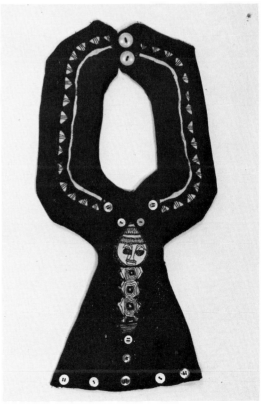

To give body to the necklace, the main shape has been cut out in triplicate—two layers of felt with a middle layer of quilting. Since felt is nonraveling, all three layers can be sandwiched together and sewn through at once. Loops for the neckline closing were made by braiding strips of felt together. These will be stitched right into the necklace.

Prints, Beads, Assemblage Necklaces

If, like Leslie Correll and Reta Miller, you have a penchant for collecting fabrics, beads, buttons, and other materials, ranging from valuables to junk, these artists' sparkling and witty assemblages should prove to be an inspiration.

Reta Miller mounted a satiny print on flowered brocade, with beads and velveteen. It's lightly stuffed. Note the artist's very effective shaping and accenting of her basic prints.

Leslie Correll calls this almost surreal combination of stuffed fabric, bone, silver, and Peking glass, Healed Heart.

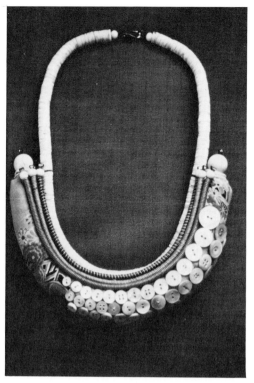

A Japanese print is combined with old buttons, telephone wire, and a clamshell. Leslie Correll.

The flap of this palm-nut collar is made with Japanese, Indonesian, and African prints. The artist, Leslie Correll, has also added mah jongg pieces, evil-eye beads, and bone.

This is a three-layered, three-way piece. Each layer can be worn independently, or all can be worn together as shown. One layer is pounded and body-formed brass, one is stuffed Indonesian batik fabric and clamshell, and one is African porcupine quills and cones. Leslie Correll.

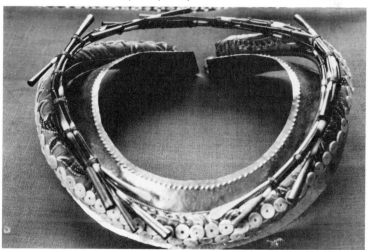

Fabric Beads

Small leaf and flower motifs are inherent in many prints. They can be used as appliqué motifs on solid-colored fabrics or independently as beads for necklaces and earrings. If used as beads, two matching shapes can be cut, stitched together, and lightly stuffed.

Leslie Correll likes the combination of hard beads and fat puffy ones made from printed fabric scraps. To make a well-sized bead:

1.   Cut a print fabric 1¾'' by 3½''.
2.   Hand- or machine-stitch the two short sides together and turn the resulting tube inside out.

Leaf shapes can be cut out in duplicate, zigzag stitched together, and lightly stuffed to make beads for necklaces, earrings, or appliqués.

The progression of one of Leslie Correll's lovely fat beads. *From left to right:* A fabric rectangle is cut, stitched on the short sides to form a tube, stuffed with Dacron, and stitched together at the open ends.

3.   Stuff the tube with cotton or Dacron.
4.   To close the open ends and form a bead shape, tuck the open edges so that they face the inside of the bead. Baste all around, drawing the basting stitches together to form a tight circle. Leave a tiny opening for the stringing wire or yarn to pass through.

A soft-hard bead necklace. The pre-Columbian beads and shells seem to have been destined for the soft batik-fabric beads. The wrapping of the neckband is done with telephone wire. Leslie Correll.

Bib Shapes Designed for a Variety of Appliqués and Uses

Most people agree that fabric jewelry is beautiful enough to hang on the wall when not in use. To give body jewelry this double use, it is time well spent to think through the basic construction in terms of this wall as well as body ornament function. For the wall ornament concept to work, specific consideration should be given to the wall hanger attachments.

We designed a bib-type necklace which, instead of buttoning or tying around the neck as such pieces usually do, was constructed to button onto a neckband with an open casing. When not in use as a necklace, a driftwood or other ornamental dowel can be slid through the casing so that the exposed ends of this hanger can rest on nails or hooks on a wall. Ideas like this tend to lead to others, in this case, the idea of convertibility from waist length to dress length.

The sample necklace was made of felt, which was cut in duplicate, with an extra layer of quilted fabric sandwiched in between. The three layers were quilt stitched in a pattern that served as a frame for the appliqués, which were made by crocheting lacy motifs out of black plastic thread around small mirrors. (See Chapter 6 for basic crochet instructions.)

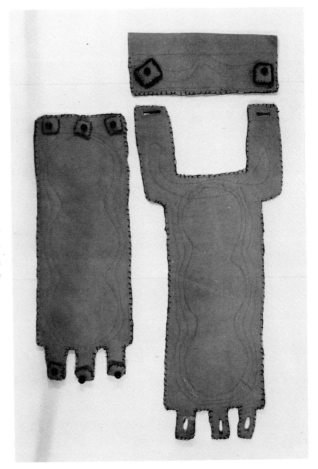

The three basic parts of the double-length, body-wall ornament. The buttons are made like little stuffed pillows. The circular quilting is stiched free-form on a sewing machine to act as a frame for the appliqués.

A second, unquilted, sample was appliquéd with felt cut to match paper snowflakes made in the popular folk art tradition of folding a square of paper in half and free-form cutting the designs. Stacked fabric layers and Yo-Yo motifs shown later in this chapter could also be effectively used, along with methods such as knotless netting, stitchery, and embroidery. Leather as a background and appliqué material can suggest a still different look.

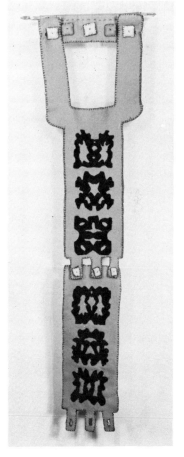

The neckpiece worn full length, appliquéd with crochet-covered mirrors.

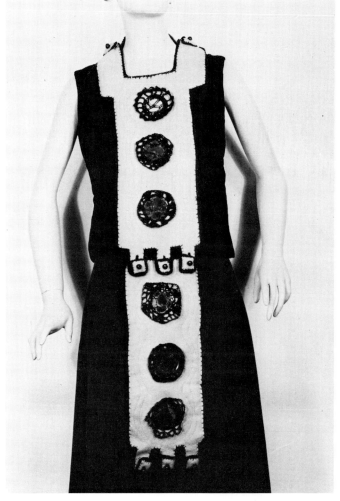

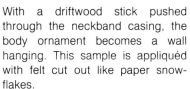

With a driftwood stick pushed through the neckband casing, the body ornament becomes a wall hanging. This sample is appliquéd with felt cut out like paper snow-flakes.

ELEGANT APPLIQUÉ

The basically simple bib shape can evolve into an elaborate piece of body jewelry with the use of elegant, richly textured fabrics like satins and velvets. Susan Morrison, who has been using fabrics as her major medium of self-expression for a dozen years, created a series of satin and velvet bibs to be worn like jewelry over very simple, nondistracting garments. The many stacked layers of fabric give the finished pieces a great relieflike quality. (Photographs by Ted Cook)

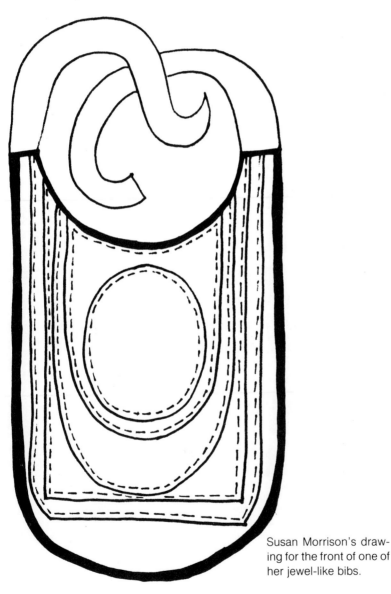

Susan Morrison's drawing for the front of one of her jewel-like bibs.

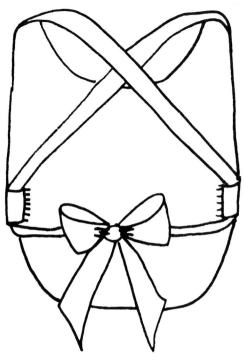

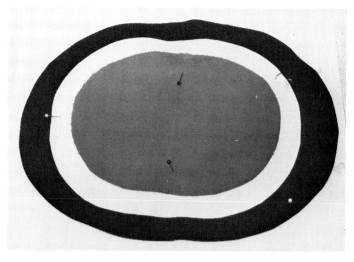

The fabrics are stacked and pinned together.

Susan's sketch for the closing ties at the back.

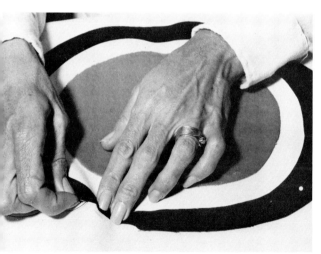

Susan likes to do most of her stitching by hand.

Bib ornament with satin streamers.

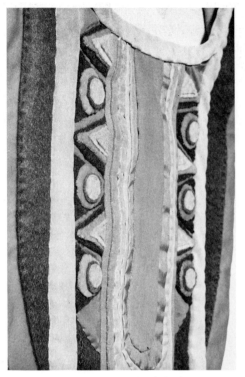

Detail view of the appliqué design.

Another of Susan's elegant body pieces.

Though most of the bibs are planned to go over very simple garments, they can on occasion be very handsome when worn with a dressy blouse.

Necklace of silver and leather encased in basketry coiled linen. The necklace has its own wall hanger. Mary Lou Higgins. Photo, Edward Higgins.

Peacock bracelet combining needlework by Betty Brown with silverwork by Maury Brown. Photo, Maury Brown.

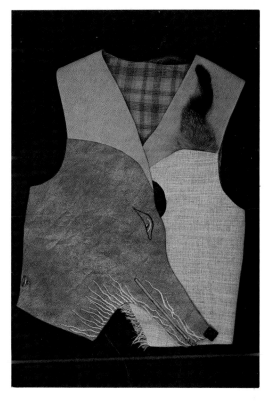

Sculptural crochet jacket with handmade buttons and hand-printed lining. Elyse Sommer.

Fox and hound fantasy vest by Sara Wolf-Soley.

Hand-painted T-shirt inspired by oil painting. T-shirt and painting, Donata Stern.

Quilted velvet necklace with hand-painted locket. The locket opens and closes. Marilyn Green.

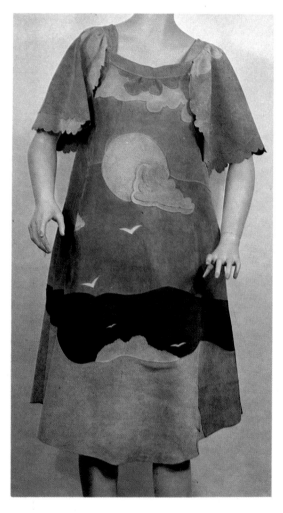

Appliquéd leather dress. John Miles.

Stacked velvet and satin bib. Susan Morrison. Photo, Ted Cook.

Panne velvet helmet with strung felt coil appliqué by Gail Stampar.

Lonely People caftan. Batik on silk by Shirley Venit Anger. Photo, E. Rosen.

Ceramic and batik pectoral by Susanna Kuo and Ginny Adelsheim.

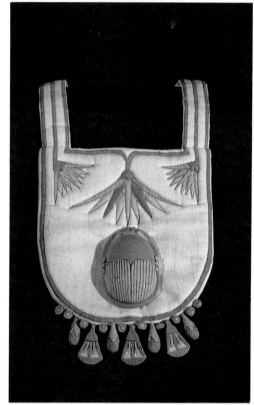

Silver brocade and cord body piece. Margaret Cusack.

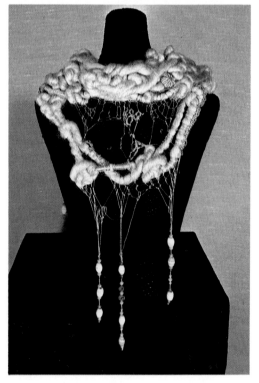

Crochet, knotless netting, and beaded body adornment on crochet-covered form. Nancy Lipe.

Portable sleeping bag in appliquéd and batiked velvets and silks with attached sleeping-waking face pillow. Gayle Feller.

Cotton appliqué cape with velvet lining and a cloisonné button by Colette. Photo courtesy artist.

Collar woven on notched cardboard loom by
Sally Davidson.

Halter woven on a painted loom by Cindy Fornari. Photo,
Dan Fornari.

Liquid-latex boa by Francie Allen.

Rear view of a corduroy jumper with detachable trapunto sun faces. Joan Schulze.

Wrapped ceremonial dance helmet. Barbara Setsu Pickett.

Velvet and brocade neckpiece with its own wall environment by Jean Boardman Knorr. Photo, Ralph Tudor.

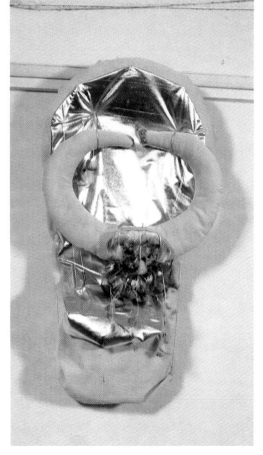

Purple Heart of Motherhood. Soft pin by Reta Miller.

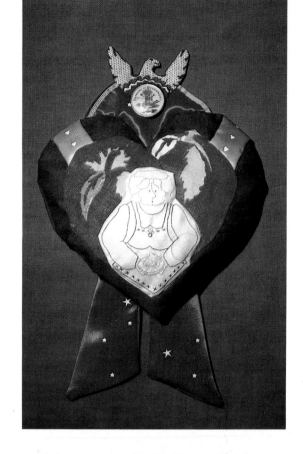

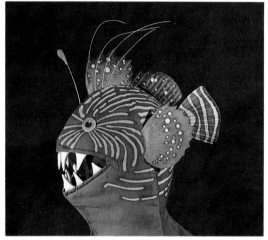

Fish helmet by Susanna Kuo. Batik on cotton organdy.

Little Chief. Body bag by Elizabeth Gurrier.

Appliquéd Clothing

California artist-designer Colette's appliquéd capes, vests, and skirts reflect her love of nature. Her landscapes are aglow with brilliant colors. Her pieces are lavishly lined in velvets and velveteens.

A rear view of one of Colette's magnificent rainbow appliqué capes.

Another of Colette's appliquéd capes, Rainbow I, owned by singer Roberta Flack.

A long skirt is appliquéd with mushrooms, deer, and a rabbit.

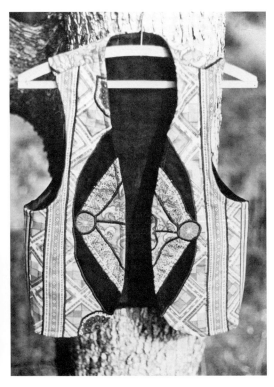

Colette's Gypsy's Vest is lined in brown velveteen.

Rear view of the Gypsy's Vest.

Reverse Appliqué

Reverse appliqué is a process of cutting through layers of fabric from top to bottom so that the colors underneath show through. This technique, as perfected and made famous by the women of San Blas, Panama, can be greatly simplified and most effective when working with nonfraying materials such as felt. The layers of fabric can be sewn all at once, with no notching or tucking under. The novice is advised to stack no more than three or four layers.

Yvonne Porcella used black, green, and yellow felt cut to conform to a paper pattern. She stuffed Dacron batting between layers of the fabric to achieve a padded effect. It all adds up to an easy and very distinctive reverse appliqué body piece. Small felt circles were appliquéd to the surface of the necklace for additional color accents.

A traditional mola design was translated into beige, brown, yellow, and pink felt. Crochet yarn, color keyed to the fabric, was added to the blanket-stitched edge. The ruffled effect of the crochet work was achieved by making lots of stitches into one. (See Chapter 6 for basic crochet instructions.)

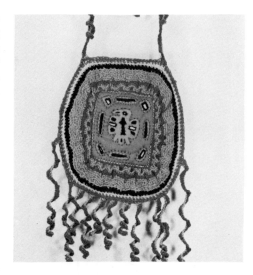

Patchwork Circles: The Shape with Unlimited Adornment Potential

Take a fabric circle about four inches in diameter, depending upon the size desired, and fold over a quarter-inch hem. Make basting stitches all around. If a nonfraying fabric like felt or soft leather is used, no folding over is necessary. Baste all around the circle and pull the basting thread to create a ruffled effect.

Popular patchwork names for these circles are Yo-Yos and rosettes. For extra weight and textural interest, insert mirrors, tin can lids, and colored wood or cardboard shapes before tightening the circle. Patchwork circles combined with yarn and beads can be strung together into an endless variety of body adornments. They can be appliquéd to garments or worn separately.

Patchwork circles of brown felt worked around torched tin-can lids and assembled into a stunning 42″ neck ornament by Bonnie Bartell. Photo, James Bartell.

Another felt patchwork piece with torched tin-can lids— this time 34″ long and combined with beads and tassels. Bonnie Bartell. Photo, James Bartell.

Easy-to-Shape Patchwork

Traditional patchwork is based upon the square-block assembly principle. Body coverings afford an opportunity to enjoy patchwork on a smaller, quicker-to-do scale. However, the body armature does inspire shapes which are curved, and piecing patches to conform to rounded rather than square or rectangular outlines can be extremely time consuming. One of the easiest ways to get around this potential roadblock is to sew a square or rectangle of patches, lay a paper pattern of the desired shape on top of the patched fabrics, and cut it out. This means cutting across sewn seams, but if very small stitches, preferably machine-made, are used there will be little or no opening of seams. In the series of photographs shown in the next pages, Sally Davidson makes a patchwork collar using this easy shaping technique. Sally used simple squares to piece her overall fabric. Other shapes and patterns, including crazy quilt piecing, could be made this way.

Print and solid fabrics will be used to create a checkerboard pattern.

A paper pattern of the planned collar shape is made, and fabric somewhat larger than the pattern is pieced together. Patchwork should be pieced a row at a time.

The pieced fabric is folded in half. The paper pattern will be pinned on top of the folded fabric, and the neckline and bottom curve cut out just as if the fabric were all in one piece from the start. Any seams which might open can be reinforced with a tacking stitch here and there, though if machine stitching, set at the smallest stitch size, is used, there will be little or no loosening of seams.

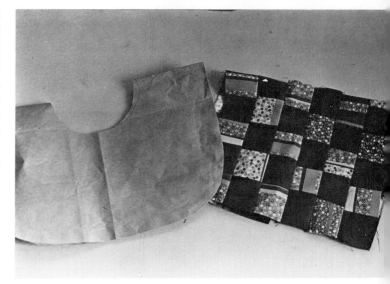

A muslin backing is sewn to the cut collar.

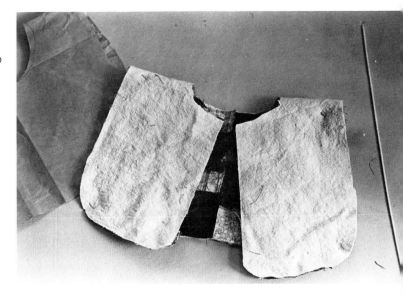

The sewing is finished.

The completed collar is embellished with buttons also used for the closing.

The finished collar.

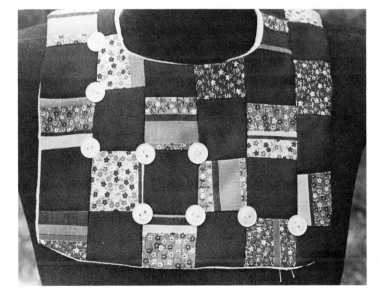

Patchwork to Make Something New from Something Old

When American pioneer women pieced and patched their marvelous quilts, their motive was strictly to make do with what they had. Fabrics in colonial America were in short supply, and every snippet and scrap was dear. Thus, though the term "recycling" is of fairly recent vintage, the idea of using and reusing materials is a time-honored tradition which lost some of its impact during the affluent 1950s and '60s. The whole trend toward creating more personalized, less status- and fashion-oriented clothing and jewelry is as much motivated by the artist-craftsman-hobbyist's involvement with ecology as his love of one-of-a-kind personal adornments.

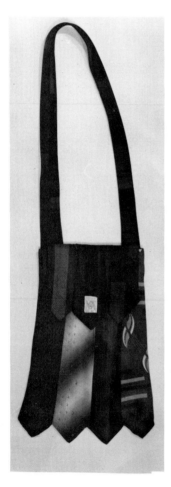

"What can you do with old ties?" If you've ever asked yourself this question, consider Reta Miller's handsome body bag. The artist has kept the label from one of the ties as a prominent part of her design, as if to say, "Sure, these are old ties, but old is as good as new!"

Yvonne Porcella salvaged a very old quilt. Even the buttons are old. Photo courtesy artist.

Rear view of Yvonne's old quilt jacket.

This dress was patched with commercial fabric. A very old mola is used for the patch pockets. The belt is patched together from old jeans. Yvonne Porcella, artist and photographer.

This magnificent patchwork dress is made from bits and pieces of fabric with special meaning for its owner, Helen Drutt. The Walking American Quilt Dress was made by Louise Todd Cope. Photo, Bob Robinson.

Arndt Tennbjerk has a "loppe marked" (Danish for flea market), and since many of the bits of lace and buttons that Louise Todd Cope used to create this cape came from there, she called her finished piece Arndt's Cape. Photo courtesy artist.

Trapunto for Appliqués, Pendants, and Buttons

One of the doll maker's favorite techniques is to stuff old sheer stockings with Dacron and then stitch through the stuffing and fabric to bring out the features. Joan Schulze works a variety of trapunto designs onto sun-shaped fabric patches. She appliqués her fat-faced suns to striking jumpers to be worn like necklaces or hung as wall hangings. By attaching the appliqués with Velcro, they retain a separate identity. Sometimes Joan uses them as neck pendants, at others as traffic-stopping bicycle clips. The faces can be used alone as one-of-a-kind buttons.

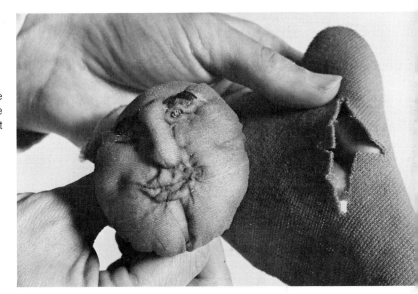

Joan Schulze inserts the doll faces into slits made into nonfraying double-knit backing fabric.

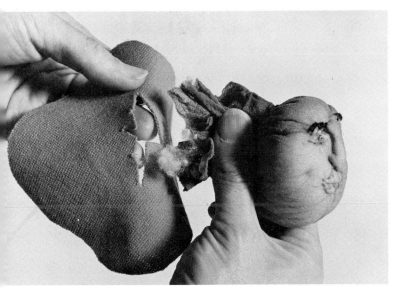

Here is a side view of the doll face, with its nylon ends being slipped into the first layer of the backing.

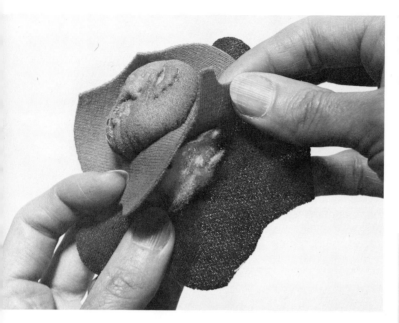

The face and top fabric layer are backed to a second layer of double-knit fabric. The nylon is spread out to avoid bulges.

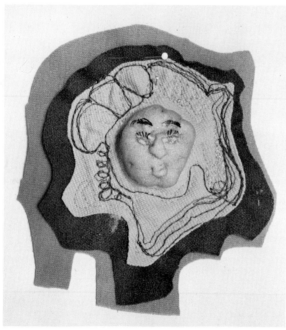

A third layer of fabric is pinned through the top two layers, ready for stitching.

Three face suns are appliquéd to the front of a beige corduroy jumper, and hung on a piece of driftwood when not worn. Joan calls her jumper Suns of Suns.

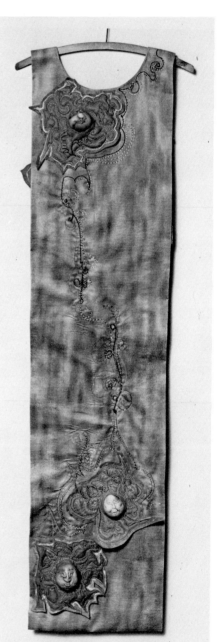

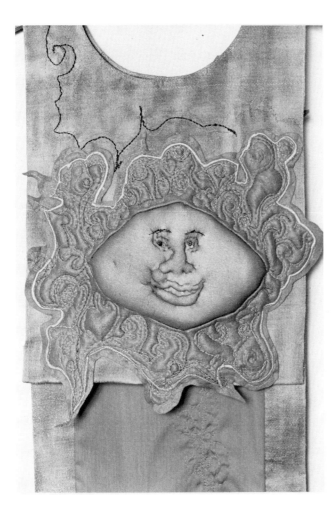

Rear view of jumper. (See color section.)

The suns are attached to the jumper with Velcro, which affords the option of wearing individual suns as neck ornaments . . .

. . . or even as bicycle clips.

Faces without the sun backing can be used as buttons.

Nancy Welch uses the trapunto button idea on Pellon, color accented with felt-tip pens.

For the man's blazer Nancy made three buttons—redhead, brunette, and blond. Unspun wool is used to create the coiffures.

Elizabeth Gurrier applies trapunto quilting to the creation of fantasy body bags.

Margaret Cusack creates an unusual piece of soft silver. Silver lamé is worked in the trapunto manner, with silver cording used to create the Medusa-like details and the closures which go around the neck and waist like a halter.

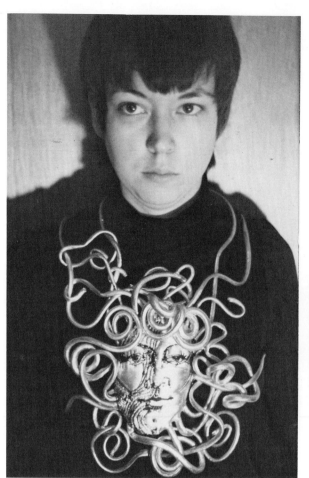

Margaret pulled some of the strings which made up the core of the silver cord to facilitate the curling of the ''hair.''

Stuffed Ornaments
with Hanging Environments

The concept of using and enjoying wearable art all the time is of special interest to those working with designs and materials intended for special-occasion wear and physically scaled so that they do not fit into the conventional jewelry box. To give her regal and distinctive neck adornments a fuller life, Jean Boardman Knorr creates unique padded and stuffed companion wall hangers. When the necklaces are joined with the environments they completely lose their wearable appearance.

A stuffed velvet ring with brocade and feathers. The ring is shaped and stuffed so that it lies around the neck without any special closure.

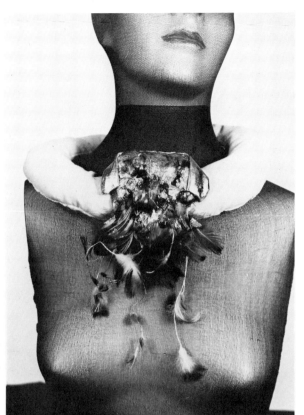

A Styrofoam board is covered with lamé and velvet. Elastic rings hold down the ends of the necklace when it becomes part of the wall environment.

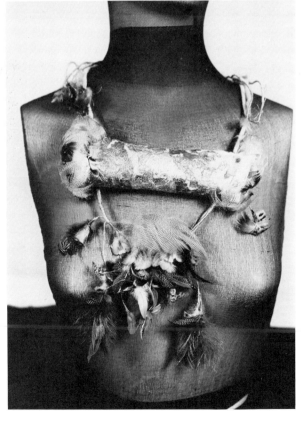

A stuffed brocade necklace with feathers and wrapping.

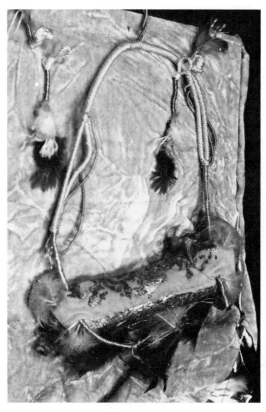

A Styrofoam board covered with crushed velvet, lamé, and feathers. Shiny cord buttons and loops are strategically placed to hold the necklace . . .

. . . when it becomes a wall sculpture.

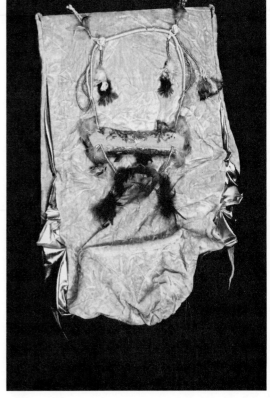

4

EMBROIDERY AND NEEDLEPOINT

Embroidery and needlepoint were long dubbed busywork for little old ladies. Monograms for handkerchiefs or canvas covers for footstools were considered typical and suitable projects. Today, though prepainted canvases and linen cloths still prevail as leisure-time projects, creative people of all ages have brought a freer and more spontaneous approach to all needlework. Stitchery groups encompassing those who do embroidery, canvaswork, and multimedia work abound throughout the country. Much of today's needlework has moved into the sphere of art, and as a result there has been some overemphasis on the strictly decorative. However, the growing interest in body adornments has reshifted the emphasis back to an appreciation of the functional. Stitchers have discovered the pleasures and satisfactions of updating the functional applications of their craft, and so thread artistry has found its way onto jeans and T-shirts as well as into jewelry forms. Machine embroidery has become as acceptable as handwork, with much mixing of the two. Yarns are used adventurously. Even gold and silver threadwork once done only by or for the very rich is now possible with the availability of lamé threads, the needleworkers' version of semiprecious silver and gold metals.

In terms of backgrounds for stitchery, anything goes. The main difference between embroidery and needlepoint is that the needlepoint stitch is worked in a mesh canvas. The stiches become part of the canvas or weave, whereas in embroidery the stitches are strictly surface decorations.

Ordinary sewing stitches, made more interesting by using yarns and colors creatively and by varying the stitch sizes, will see the novice through initial projects. The one all-purpose canvaswork stitch is a slanted one much like the overhand sewing stitch or half-cross stitch known in needlepoint jargon as the tent or Continental stitch. Many excellent books and booklets clearly illustrating the many stitches used by advanced needleworkers are available. We refer those who want to build their own stitching vocabulary to some of those listed in the Bibliography.

Stitchery, especially when worked in fine threads, is not for those in a hurry. However, you don't have to do a lot when working with body adornments. Patches of color can turn ordinary scarves into extraordinary head, neck, and waist adornments. Bits of thread, beads, and fabrics can transform the remains of a pair of denim pants into versatile, double-duty body pieces. Heavier knitting, crocheting, and weaving yarns of course cover more fabric and build up texture faster than thin cotton and novelty threads.

Patches of delicate embroidery can turn ordinary scarves into extraordinary head coverings. Ahuvah Bebe Dushey. Photo, Kahane/Kirshner, Image I.

Embroidery is used to create a decorative medallion on an old crocheted beret. Ahuvah Bebe Dushey. Photo, Kahane/Kirshner, Image I.

Bits of thread and beads are used to recycle denim from discarded pants into handsome necklaces. Ahuvah Bebe Dushey. Photo, Kahane/Kirshner, Image I.

Ahuvah Bebe Dushey used her stitchery talents to transform old denim pants legs into body pieces that could be worn as a halter or . . .

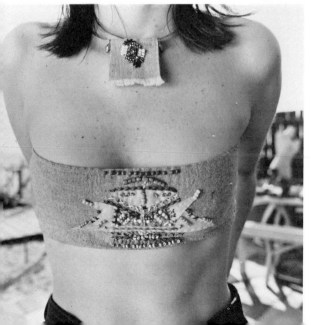

. . . as a waist adornment. Photo, Kahane/Kirshner, Image I.

Another double-duty embroidered denim adornment by Ahuvah Bebe Dushey. Here felt and beads accent a pretty neck . . .

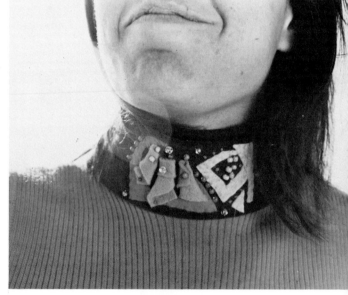

. . . and here the same piece functions handsomely as a headband. Photo, Kahane/Kirshner, Image I.

The ubiquitous denim jacket serves as a handsome background for Jan Lankenau's free-form embroidery.

Wool yarns worked in large, bold designs go fast enough to cover larger areas such as Bonnie Bartell's lovely handmade petal dress. The beaded wool tassels accent the texture of the embroidery.

Marilyn Motz uses embroidery couching to create bright and sporty embroidered neck-pieces.

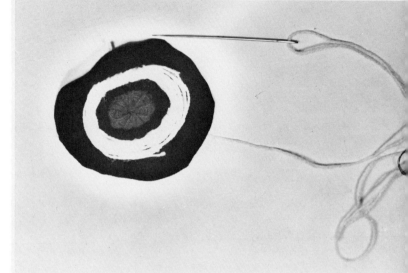

Marilyn couches rows of different-colored yarns onto a backing of felt . . .

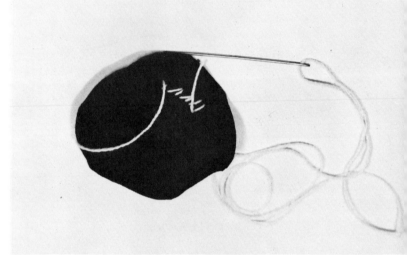

. . . carrying the threads across the back of the material.

Soft Jewels: Gold, Silver, and Other Glitter

Today the high cost of real gold thread materials, rather than the class restrictions imposed in medieval times, makes their use too costly for general use. Few modern American craftsmen work in genuine gold-thread embroidery, though in England there are still numerous embroiderers working in real gold, many doing ecclesiastic commission work. Many good-quality lamé threads and fabrics are available which give all craftspeople an opportunity to create truly elegant soft jewelry without having to expend formidable sums on material. Silks, bits of fur, and colored Mylar can all be used to create glittering stitched jewels. The necklaces of Jean Boardman Knorr on pages 71 and 72 and Margaret Cusack's silver trapunto body adornment on page 70 are further examples of the use of these materials.

Bucky King works in both real gold and the less costly craft lamés. Much of her gold threadwork is commissioned and may be seen in traveling exhibitions throughout Europe. With the high cost of real gold, Bucky saves every bit of scrap and often combines genuine gold leftovers with a variety of what she calls junk.

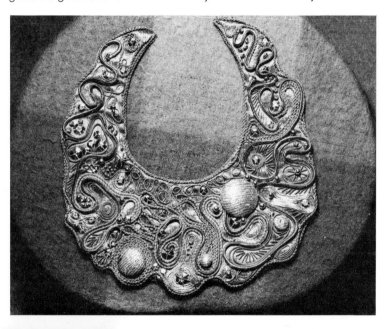

An all-gold collar in metal thread embroidery. Bucky King.

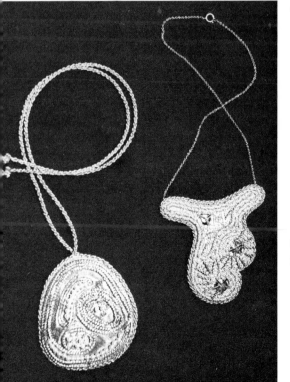

Gold thread embroidery pendants with some real and some not-so-real gold. Bucky King.

Gold thread embroidery necklace.
Bucky King.

Mary Rhodes, one of England's experts in fine needlework, uses traditional canvas and embroidery work to create a distinctly modern necklace. It is worked in blue and green silk on a background of gold and silver metallic thread. Photo courtesy *Embroidery* magazine.

Joan Schulze combines embroidery, quilting, and wrapping in this small but important soft jewel. Silk is embroidered, beaded, and quilted. The hanging part of the pendant consists of wool threads wrapped with Mexican floss for a shiny look. (See Chapter 5 for wrapping instructions and techniques.) Feathers and fur complete the opulent look.

Helen Bitar's brilliant stitcheries are not usually designed to be worn. Nevertheless, many of her small hangings are shaped so that they can be worn like pendants. Helen works with clusters of brocade, lamé threads, and found objects. Anyone using intricate work like this and delicate materials is advised to make the embroidered ornaments detachable, using either snaps or Velcro.

Mylar with Embroidery

Betty Brown uses a variety of materials to add sparkle and contrast to her embroidery. She particularly likes to use colored Mylars. In the pendant illustrated, Betty cut two circles out of cerise and purple Mylar. She punched holes all around with a leather punch, though a paper punch would work too. A padding of polyester was worked in between the Mylar circle and then a row of buttonhole stitches was made around the edge, using thread to match the Mylar. Sometimes Betty adds small lead washers to the stuffing for extra weight. The stitchery consists of a web or yarn sewn across the face of each side of the circle. This web is filled in with thread woven over and under the spokes. Decorative embroidery stitches around the edge of the pendants, some beads, and a crochet chain neckband complete the necklace.

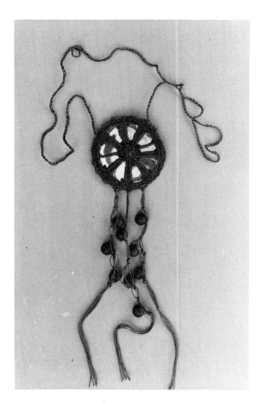

Close-up of stitchery detail of Mylar necklace.

Mylar necklace with embroidery. Betty Brown. Photo, Maury Brown.

Stained-Glass Embroidery

Using gold-colored silk and black rattail cord, Betty Brown created a soft pendant with a stained-glass look. To add firmness and body she inserted a piece of plastic cut from the lid of a container. She started her design by embroidering the rattail leading and then filled in the leaded areas with different-colored silk threads worked in a couched grid pattern. When the embroidery was finished, the shape was cut out and embroidered around the outside. The neck chain, which was knotted, could also be knitted, crocheted, or wrapped.

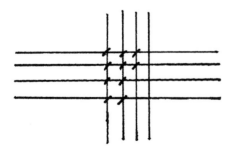

Sketch of couched grid pattern for stained-glass necklace.

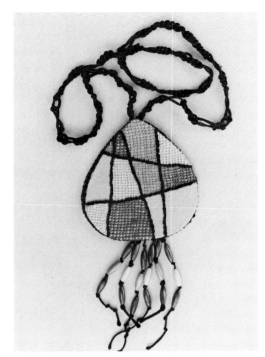

"Stained-glass" embroidery necklace. Betty Brown. Photo, Maury Brown.

Rear view of "stained-glass" necklace.

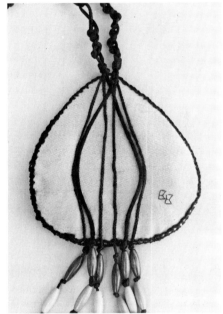

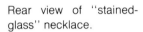

Embroidery Belt with Needlepoint Buckle

Embroidery and needlepoint combine beautifully into a single, sensational body piece, as illustrated by Robbie Fanning. Robbie chose the shape of a butterfly for her needlepoint buckle so that she could use color and form to show the metamorphosis of a butterfly (ovum–larva–pupa–imago). Her machine-embroidered belt was planned in a muted gray to explode into the brilliant colors of the butterfly. (Photographs courtesy artist.)

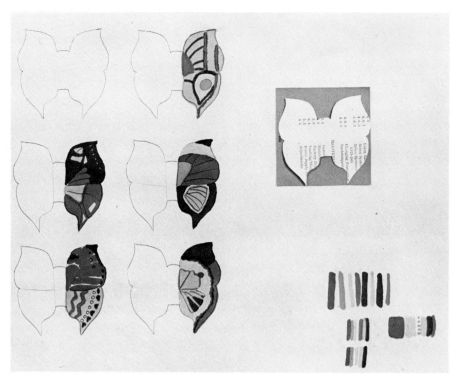

A template has been made of the basic butterfly shape and various colors of designs are tried out with marking pens.

Materials for making the butterfly have been chosen and laid out: wool, raffia in several shades, perle cotton, mohair, tatting cotton, bouclé, wool and glass jewels. Number 12 mono canvas has been marked with the butterfly outline.

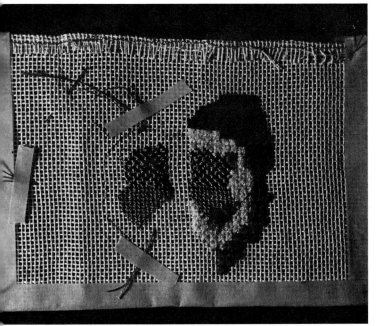

The canvas has been bound with masking tape (one side had already been turned up and zigzagged on the machine) and the butterfly is now half-stitched. Robbie begins her stitches from the front of the canvas, leaving a short tail on the back which is covered up as the stitching progresses. Eventually, the tail is pulled through to the back and cut up. When tails get in the way, bits of tape hold them out of the working area.

When the butterfly is completed, an interfacing of stiff belting is cut to fit, the canvas is trimmed to the butterfly shape, curves are clipped, and edges turned over the belting and basted in place. A backing of green velveteen is cut to fit and a binding stitch is worked all around the shape. Before the entire binding is finished, a small bit of padding is pushed inside.

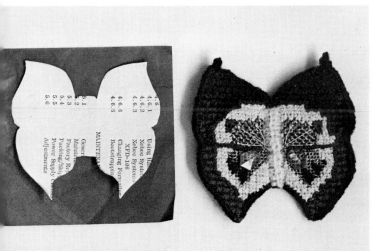

Here is the finished butterfly buckle next to the original template, showing how a design evolves and changes.

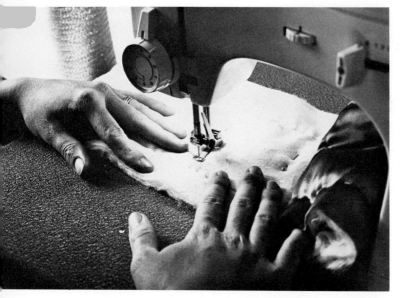

The fabric for the belt is lightly padded and backed with muslin. After basting the layers together along the edges of the belt, trace the design onto the muslin with a pencil. Heavy gray and silver thread were wound onto the bobbin with the tensions adjusted so that when worked with the wrong side up, the gray thread lay on the surface of the gray material as if couched. The design was worked in free machine embroidery.

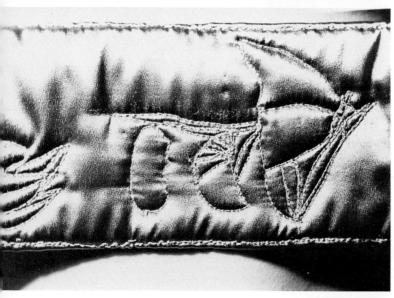

Close-up of the finished machine stitching.

The finished belt.

Soft-Hard: Petit Point and Silver

Just as needlepoint and embroidery can be combined, so needlepoint and more traditional jewelry materials work well together. In Chapter 2 we saw an example of two sisters merging their skills with batik and ceramics. In the sketches and photographs that follow we see a husband and wife, Maury and Betty Brown, bring her needlepoint and his silversmithing talents into a harmonious whole. The peacock design was planned so that the chased surface of the silver would give the impression of feather growth along the petit-point quill in the eye of the peacock feather.

Betty and Maury work from carefully planned preliminary sketches. Betty transfers her graph-paper sketch directly to canvas (Mono #18) using waterproof needlepoint markers. Maury cuts from a flat piece of sterling the silver piece which will frame the central needlepoint motif, and then chases the feather texture and form. Betty works her needlepoint, the Continental stitch, onto the flat canvas *before* cutting the bracelet shape. The bracelet shape is cut with a ¼-inch border which can be folded under. The edges around the curve are notched before folding it for a smooth edge.

The silver is formed over a mandrel, then buffed, polished, and cemented to the canvas with epoxy cement. The canvas edges are folded and fastened by stitching back and forth across the piece. The edge of the canvas attached to the silver is glued. The back of the bracelet is finished with a ribbon sewn over the folded edges, and Velcro is used as a fastener. To protect the needlepoint against soiling and wear, the silver is masked off and the canvas sprayed with Scotchgard. (Photographs, Maury Brown.)

Maury working on the silver and Betty on petit point for a petit-point-and-silver bracelet.

The materials used for the bracelet. Betty and Maury both work from carefully planned sketches.

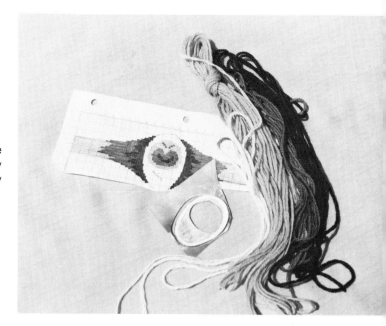

Patterns and tools for the silver work.

The petit point is done on canvas before it is cut and shaped.

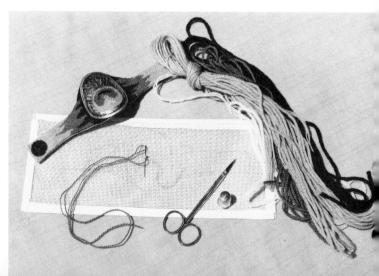

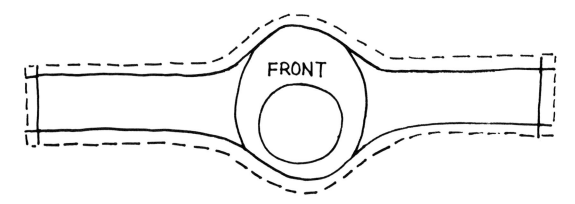

Sketch showing the cutting of the canvas, with border allowance for folding under edges.

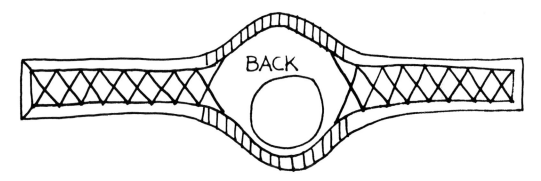

Sketch showing Betty's method of stitching back and forth across the back of the canvas.

Betty made another sketch to show how she completed the back of the bracelet, adding a ribbon backing and two Velcro dots for easy closing.

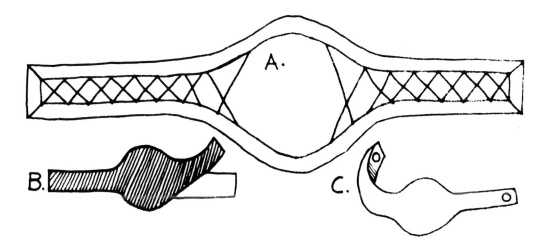

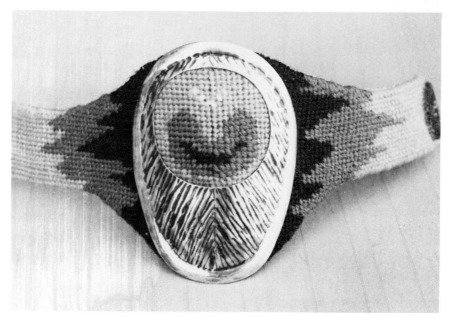

Peacock bracelet in petit point and silver.

Traditional Needlepoint Reshaped

Those who love the look of fine old needlepoint but lack the patience to work with it can be creative by updating the shape and function of old or worn pieces.

An old needlepoint bag with a broken catch and a frayed bottom was recycled by cutting the canvas from the front and back of the bag and shaping these pieces into a neck ornament. Each piece of needlepoint was edged with blanket stitches in green yarn to match one of the shades of green in the needlepoint. This edging was then built up with crochet worked off the blanket stitches. The crochet serves to connect the three parts of the necklace. (See Chapter 6 for crochet instructions.)

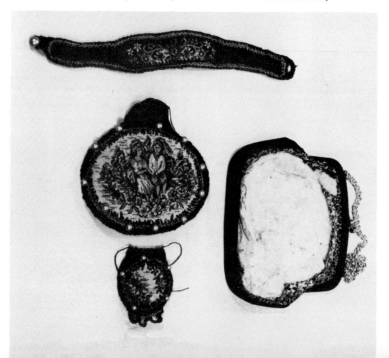

Recycled petit point necklace with crochet and beads.

Just as old petit point can be utilized for body ornaments, so can bits of lace be embroidered onto clothing and accessories, instead of actually doing one's own lace embroidery. This lace-and-bead embroidered dress with matching purse is a lovely example. Photo, James Bartell.

A capelet, also embroidered with lace and beads, completes the dress. Photo, James Bartell.

5

WRAPPED AND COILED ORNAMENTS

Wrapping and coiling are traditional basketry techniques. In recent years, more and more craftspeople have discovered potentials beyond basketry for these easy-to-learn methods. The soft-art jeweler has replaced the more typical basketry materials such as reeds and grasses with colorful yarns. Wire, plastic tubing, wrapping, and laundry cord have become viable wrapping cores.

The application of basketry methods to jewelry is especially appealing for those not inclined to spend the time required for conventional basketry work. Wrapping and coiling also work well as wearables because they cling and conform to the body, without confining or restricting. Wrapped and coiled adornments have body and yet are light in weight. Their forms can be simple, or bold and brilliant. Unlike crochet and weaving, where good-quality yarns are an important consideration if one wants high-quality results, wrapping and coiling tend to look great even with the least-expensive knitting worsteds.

The design potential for wrapped and coiled ornaments is truly limitless. The most inexperienced craftsperson seems able to envision color and shapes easily. This is one craft that quickly breaks down those "I'm not creative" mental blocks so many people have. Wrapping and coiling can be learned by young children. Moreover, teachers of older people should consider using these methods. We have seen people whose weakening eyesight makes very close work difficult respond with enormous enthusiasm to this "new" craft.

Nonfiber objects can be incorporated into wrapped work, making it a valuable adjunct craft for ceramists, silversmiths, enamelers, and so on. Other fiber crafts such as crochet, macramé, and weaving can be teamed with wrapping and coiling, as will be seen in later chapters. In fact, the terminology of wrapping and coiling is that of the weaver: the core is usually referred to as the warp, the wrapping yarn as the weft.

Materials Needed for Wrapping and Coiling

No special tools are needed. Most people will have the makings of at least a few beginning projects right at hand—clothesline, wrapping cord, spool or other lightweight wire, and yarns. The only tools needed are an embroidery needle and a pair of scissors.

The Basic Method

Basically, wrapping consists of wrapping fiber around other fibers. The fiber to be wrapped (the core or warp) should be fairly firm. It can consist of laundry rope, raffia, jute, or a number of yarns bundled together. Wire, ranging from lightweight spool wire to fairly sturdy aluminum, can be worked into the warp for an extremely solid yet flexible and easy-to-manipulate core.

The wrapping fiber, or weft, is usually a single strand and should be no longer than three feet. It is much easier to add new weft than to try to manipulate awkwardly long lengths of yarn. It is possible to wrap long lengths of a core and then twist the finished wrap into a desired form, tacking down the coils thus formed with a sewing needle and thread matching the wrapping yarn. Coils can also be formed by wrapping the core, bending it as one goes along, and using the weft yarn to connect portions of the coil. A demonstration for making a basic coil follows.

Making a Basic Wrapped Coil

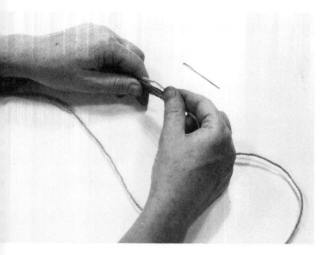

Start the coil with a warp core of multiple strands of acrylic rug yarn. Use a 3-foot length of yarn for your weft or wrapping yarn and lay this over the core, about 1½'' from the end.

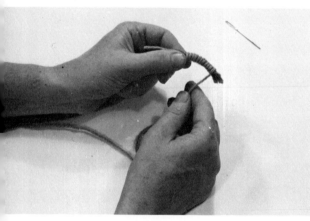

Wrap the core tightly to the end.

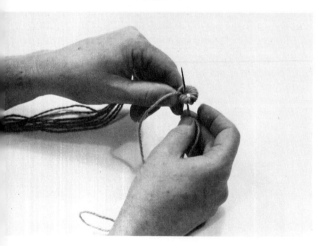

Bend the end over and thread the weft onto an embroidery needle. Bring this through the center of the loop which has been formed.

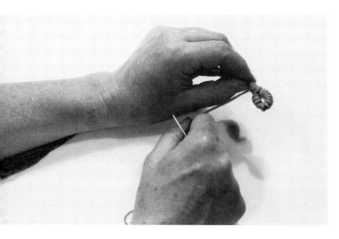

Continue wrapping around the warp until you are ready to bend it to build the coil shape.

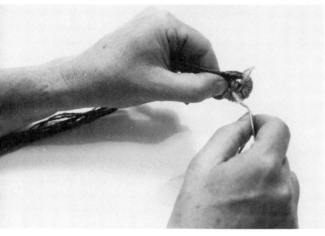

Now bring the wrap around the back and up through the center.

Bring the needle over and under as shown, and continue wrapping in a back-to-front wrapping pattern.

These two steps are repeated either in a regular pattern of bringing the needle over and under the coil after a set number of winds, or in an irregular pattern.

To add new weft, cut a new length of yarn and lay it along the core as you did to start the coil. Wind the new weft around the core and the leftover weft end. Continue wrapping and coiling as before. If you are changing the weft to add a new color, you can carry the old color along the back. Feathers and beads can be wrapped in as you go along.

If you work on a large piece and run out of wrap core, the old and new warp should be spliced together. This can be done by unraveling ends of fibers and twisting the beginnings and ends together (a dab of white glue is helpful) or by tying the ends together with a bit of fine spool wire as shown. (Always wrap extrafirmly where a new core connection has been made.)

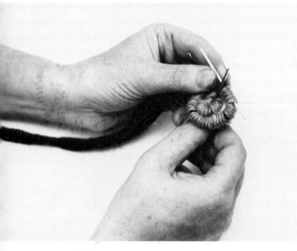

To end off a coil, hold a round toothpick (or an embroidery needle, thin knitting needle, or the like) along the last part of the core being wrapped. When you finish wrapping, remove the toothpick.

Bring the threaded weft needle up through the center of the coil to secure it and then push it through the toothpick-loosened wrap. Pull tight. Both weft and warp ends can now be cut and still remain securely fastened.

Coil Adornments

Once you know how to make a basic wrapped coil you can create a rich assortment of one-of-a-kind adornments. Variations in color, texture, and use can be achieved through the selection of materials, the addition of feathers and beads, and the way you form the coils.

Louise Robbins uses a warp of natural linen and Greek wool for her wrapping. Her coiled forms are wearable as pendants or hair or ear ornaments. She wraps marabou feathers, bits of bone, and silver into the end of her forms.

The triangle design of this simple coil was worked by carrying orange yarn in back of the predominantly natural coil. The weft was changed to the carried-along orange whenever the triangle area was reached. Marabou feathers were wrapped into the ends of the warp, which were left loose.

Here is the same basic coil-with-triangle pattern, this time with the coil shaped to form a little cup shape.

Louise lets her flat coil meander into free-form loops. These earrings as well as the other forms could be used interchangeably as pendants, belt dangles, or collar adornments.

More Wrapped Adornments

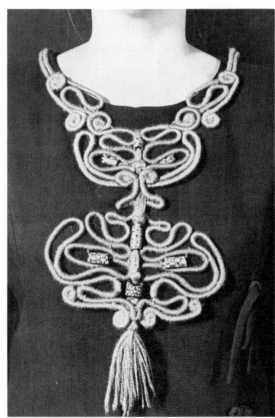

Jeanne Lowe wrapped this beautiful necklace in three sections. She used 3/16'' nylon cording for her core and Persian wool tapestry yarns for her weft. The yarn-and-African-trade-bead section was interwined down the center.

This vestlike adornment was designed by Louise Robbins for Carvel Van Der Burch. Greek wool is wrapped with silk and accented with feathers and silver Mexican miracle charms called milagros.

Wrapping can be used to achieve ethereal effects, as exemplified by this unusual vest of wrapped linen threads and abacus beads by Louise Todd Cope.

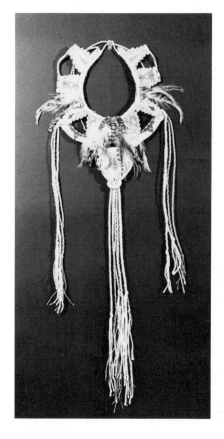

Hilda Duffek's collar necklace is braided and coiled with braided fringes.

A very mod body covering results when solid, thick cores are wrapped with bright colors plus chunky wooden beads. Photo courtesy Coats & Clark.

An example of chunky wraps, by Marilyn Motz.

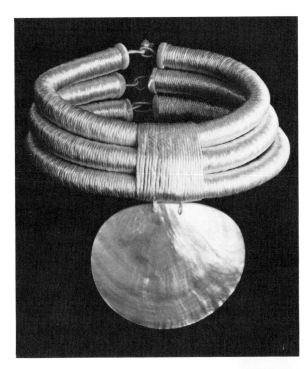

More chunky cores, here with a superelegant approach through the use of satiny wrappings and a glowing shell pendant. Susan Green. Photograph, I. O'Leary.

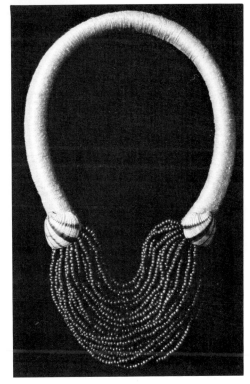

To go with her wrapped linen neck-band, Susan Green used about a kilo of glass beads. Photo, Baron Wolman.

Wire Cores for Flexible Shapes and Closures

As mentioned, wire facilitates wrapping and adds to the flexibility of the shape. Experiment with different weights of wire. The chief advantage of this type of wrapping is that the wrapped lengths can be easily twisted into sturdy, form-holding shapes. The core ends can be easily twisted together.

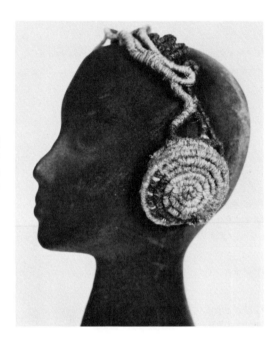

Aluminum wire is used for the core of these earmuff baskets so that the ear cups could be adjusted to fit over the wearer's ear. Handspun and hand-dyed rug yarn is used for the wrap.

Wrapped Aluminum-Core Necklace

Red, pink, yellow, gold, and acrylic wool are wrapped over aluminum wire and yarn in a random color pattern. The ends of the wire portion of the core are twisted together and covered with wrapping.

The long wrapped circle is twisted together.

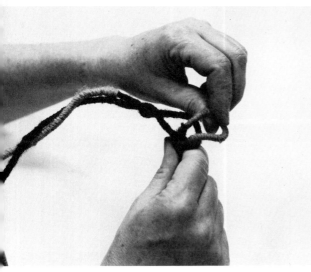

The end loops are twisted and bent into an easy closure.

The necklace can be worn as shown, or a decorative wrapped and fringed pendant can be added.

Wrapped and Fringed Pendants
with Coil-Button Accents

Yarns of different colors have been bundled together and folded in half around the center of the aluminum-wrapped necklace. A separate yarn core is started and . . .

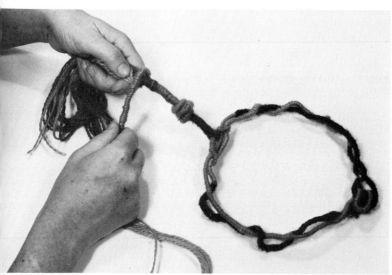

. . . tied onto the central wrapping . . .

. . . two or three times. The ends of the core are left to hang down and become part of the main core.

The coil buttons can be left with the coiled ridges showing, or the warp can be brought over and under the separate coils to produce a smooth beadlike button.

The necklace is complete. Many variations in shape, color, and texture are possible with this basic procedure.

Jean Boardman Knorr also likes the look of fat yarn accents. She makes her "beads" by winding small balls of wool, then works yarn all around the basic ball, like a coil. The coils are stitched down as she goes along.

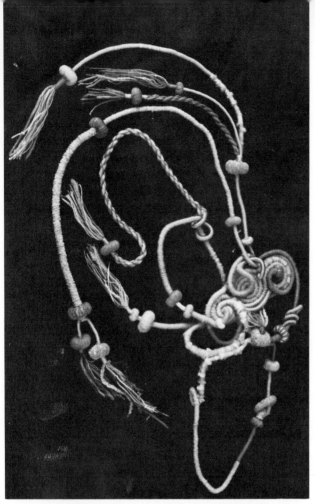

In this triple-threat necklace, Madge Copeland combines wrapping, coiling, and braiding with fat-coil button accents.

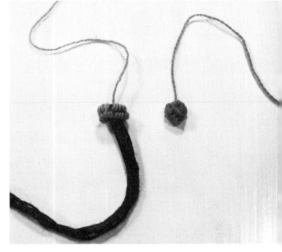

Yarn coil button-bead shapes can be made and used separately. The core can be allowed to fall out of the center like a fringe as at left or securely tied off with spool wire and cut, leaving only the weft as a thread to sew on the button.

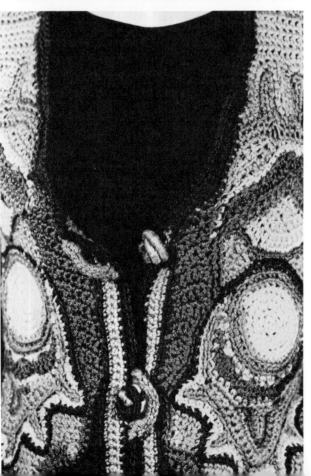

Wrapped and coiled buttons add a perfect decorative touch to a crocheted jacket.

Wrapped and coiled button shapes
appliquéd to a velvet nonfitted vest.
Jean Boardman Knorr.

Soft-Yarn Beads

Very soft yarn beads—puffs more than beads—can be made by
bundling many lengths of yarn, wrapping them tightly at spaced
intervals, and letting the nonwrapped areas puff out.

Yarn can be wound around 4 T-pins pushed into a polyfoam board or several thicknesses of corrugated cardboard. Thin, sturdy thread is tightly wrapped at regular or irregular intervals.

The yarn puffs up into soft beads.

Bundles of yarn can also be wrapped onto a wire neckband as shown.

The puffiness was accented by using a dog-grooming comb to tease the wool into fatter, more solid puffs.

Wrapped Cardboard Cores

Bea Miller makes a wrapped necklace using a flat cardboard core cut to a desired shape. One side of the cardboard is covered with white glue. Then the yarn is carefully wrapped around the glue-covered background. This easy method gives most-attractive results.

A cardboard-wrapped necklace. Bea Miller.

Another cardboard-wrapped necklace. Bea Miller.

A Mixed-Media Approach
to Coiled Body Adornments

In this final demonstration, Mary Lou Higgins brilliantly affirms our belief that a craftsman's creative strength lies not just in the determination to learn one craft well but in the courage and enterprise to master several, plus the vision to consolidate seemingly diverse skills into a unified whole. Mary Lou is well versed in ceramics, weaving, basketry, and crochet. She decided to combine her painted ceramics with basketry and coiling.

Mary Lou worked with a double strand of fiber plus a single one of spool wire for a firm and flexible core. She used wool for her wrapping. In order to encase her ceramic discs firmly, she made a hole at the top before firing. Enamels, wood pieces—anything requiring an interesting frame—could be similarly encased. (Photographs, Edward Higgins)

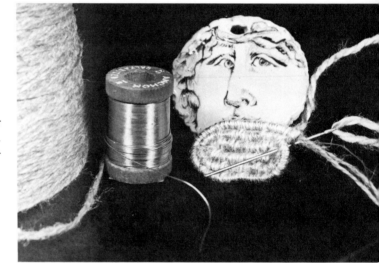

A coil is started which will cover the back of the ceramic disc. Mary Lou Higgins. Photos, Edward Higgins.

When the back of the ceramic area is covered, the needle is passed through the opening at the top of the ceramic piece and the wrapping is continued, close to the edge. If an object to be encased has not been prepared with a hole, the wrapping will hold without this extra security, or else a dab of glue can be applied to the back of the insert.

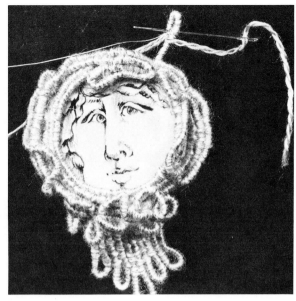

As the coil builds up, the wrapping is worked over the edge of the ceramic drawing.

The wrapping now progresses in a more free-form manner, with loops and curls and open areas created at random.

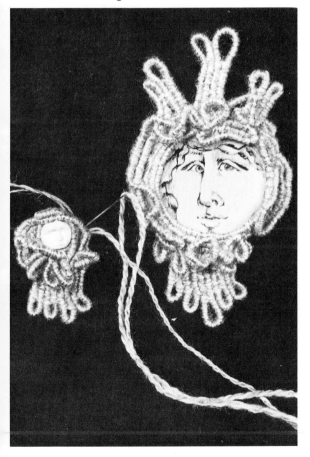

After the main piece is completed, a smaller addition is started, this time using a small porcelain head.

A second porcelain head is started. Bronze droplets which Mary Lou forged and drilled with African beads are wired to the bottom of the central pendant.

The completed forms are wrapped together. Extra bronze and beads are added to reinforce the form.

To give her stunning necklace a double life, Mary Lou wrapped heavy wire and twisted it into a decorative wall hanger.

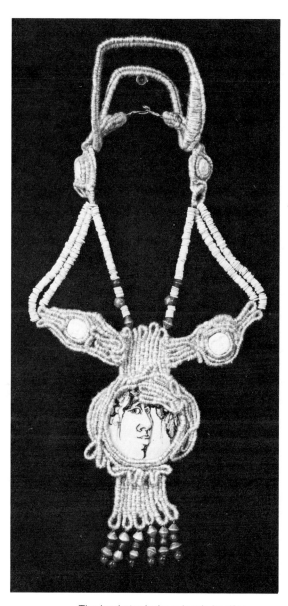

The basic technique lends itself to many arrangements. Here long strands of shell hishi are used instead of some of the wrapping of the previously shown necklace.

Mary Lou mounts etched sterling on black leather (the silver is adhered to the leather with epoxy) and the results are equally effective. Practically anything could be combined with this type of coiling and wrapping.

6

CREATIVE CROCHET

Although crochet has a long tradition as a popular handicraft, its possibilities as a free and creative form of self-expression have only begun to be explored since the late 1960s. The realization that crochet need not be worked in the usual row-on-row, bottom-to-top sweater fashion but can grow more naturally when shape is built onto shape has had a marked effect upon all crochet work. By using paper clothing patterns as shaping guides, crocheters have been enabled to work out designs as do painters, doing some planning by means of presketching designs, or letting things happen as they go along.

Experimentation with stitches has led to the discovery that crochet lends itself to three-dimensional effects. For example, simply by making many stitches in one space, wonderful sculptural ruffles can result. Forms can be built by working right on top of a base piece. The general interest in all fiber crafts and the resulting increase in the availability of unusual yarns has also had its effect upon the look of crochet.

Interestingly, even as more and more crocheters have become involved with free-form creative crochet, the traditional lacy look once associated with all crochet work has enjoyed continued popularity, for this is one of those rare crafts not subject to trends. Instead, each new crochet discovery is added to traditional methods, rather than replacing them. Thus, a classic lacy crochet collar can be reinterpreted into a distinctly new and modern use.

Lace collar from
*Farm and Home
Journal,* circa 1880.

Bucky King uses gold wire with
linen in a modern version of the
old-fashioned lace collar.

Although there is enough to say about crochet stitches and techniques to fill up an entire book, as our own *A New Look at Crochet,* those interested in creating artistic, distinctive body adornments can do so with the most minimal skills. The single crochet stitch can see you through the making of necklaces, hats, and clothing. The ability to work in circular as well as straight-up-and-down patterns will provide the flexibility needed for interesting designs and effects. The demonstrations of stitches and techniques presented here will get the beginner started.

Starting to Crochet

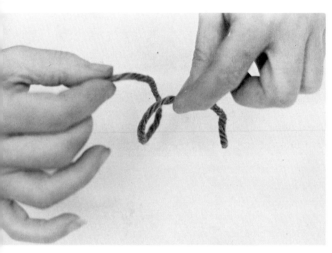

All crochet work starts with a slipknot made by holding the short end of the yarn in the left hand and bringing the long end around the loop as shown.

Let the long end of the yarn form a vertical bar across the loop and pull it through the hook. When this loop is tightened (but not too tightly), you are ready to begin a basic crochet chain.

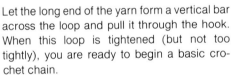

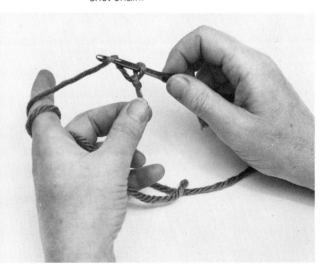

Bring the yarn in front of the loop on the hook and pull it through. Repeat this step until you have a chain of the desired length.

Thick chains made from 9 strands of knitting worsted, 6½ yards long each, are pinned parallel to one another onto a board. Contrast-colored yarn is threaded onto an embroidery needle and wrapped back and forth between the two chains to produce a loose, fluffy band.

The crochet chain alone can serve as a basis for simple and colorful yarn adornments. Try chaining long lengths of six to nine strands of yarn into a fat chain with flowing tassel ends. The chains can be one color or multicolored and used as belts or headbands. Two of the chains can be pinned to a pressboard or foam board and used as holding cords through which to thread coreless wraps of contrasting yarns. Marilyn Motz used this technique to make a collar for an ornament that can double as a cape or skirt.

Marilyn Motz has used a thick double chain with loose wrapping to act as a tie-on neckband for a capelike body ornament. Long multiple strands of yarn are added to the collar, with intermittent areas of wrapping added for design interest. Two single-strand crochet chains connect the flowing parts of the cape and act as closing ties.

The loose chain ends of the collar are large enough to fit around the waist so that the cape can be transformed into an apronlike skirt.

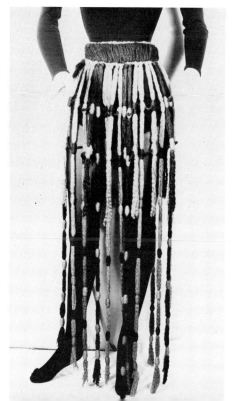

The Single Crochet Stitch

This is the all-purpose basic stitch. Other stitches are really not new or different but are variations of this single crochet.

To start, always insert your hook into the stitch next to the loop. In the photograph, the hook has been removed so the reader can clearly see where to begin. The slipknot at the base is not counted as a stitch.

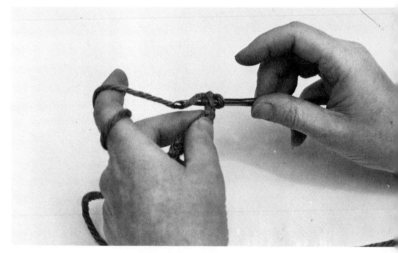

Begin the stitch by inserting the hook and bringing the yarn in front of it. Pull through the first loop . . .

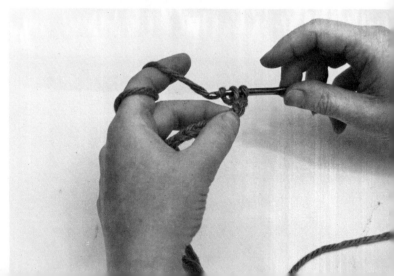

. . . yarn over again and through the remaining loop. Every crochet stitch ends with a single loop on the hook.

When you have worked across the row, an extra chain must be made. This is called a turning chain, and is counted as the first stitch of the next row.

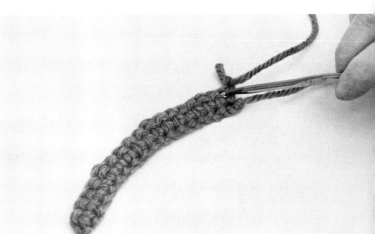

Here is the work turned for another row. The hook points to the chain next to the turning chain, which is always the starting place for a new row.

Other Stitches

The half-double and double crochet stitches are merely taller versions of the single crochet stitch.

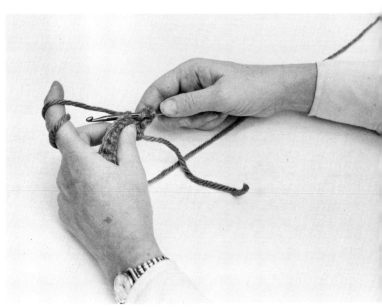

For the half-double crochet, make two chains before you turn. Bring the yarn over *before you insert the hook*.

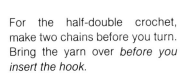

Yarn over in front of the three loops on the hook and pull through all three loops to complete the stitch.

To make a double crochet, make *three* chains to turn, and repeat the first step of the double crochet. However, after you bring the yarn over before the three loops, pull through only *two* loops, so that two loops remain on the hook. Bring the yarn over before the two remaining loops as shown, and yarn through to complete the stitch.

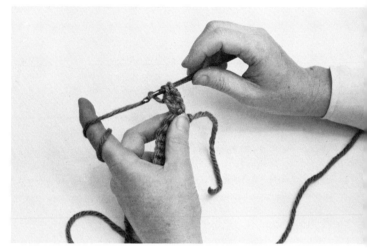

Even taller stitches, such as the treble crochet, can be made by forming a turning chain of four stitches, bringing the yarn over twice before the loop, and then working off the loops in pairs, three times, until the usual single loop remains. By being able to make stitches of varying heights, the crocheter can create gradations in the shape of the fabric. Shapes can be narrowed by decreasing the height and widened by increasing it. To decrease the height, skip a stitch; to increase it, go twice into a stitch. To create puffs or ruffles, go several times into a stitch.

Three-Dimensional Effects

To create three-dimensional sculptural effects, insert your hook right into the surface of the crochet work and make single crochet stitches in any direction. Ahuvah Bebe Dushey's necklace bag illustrates the results which can be achieved by using only a single crochet stitch, letting some of the stitches rove on top of the base to create a sculptural pattern.

 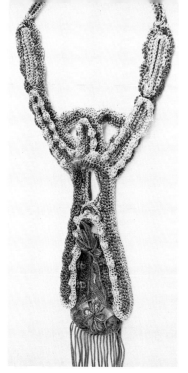

A necklace bag constructed of a basic rectangle in all-single-crochet stitches. Single crochets are worked onto the flap in a random pattern to add color and a three-dimensional effect. Ahuvah Bebe Dushey. Photo, Kahane/Kirshner, Image I.

Mona Costa started this sculptural neckpiece with some antique gold-lace motifs bought in a lace and trimmings store. She crocheted all around with lamé thread, adding ruffles and oval shapes to the surface. Photo, Kent D. Costa.

Round Shapes

Being able to work in the round greatly expands the range of things to be crocheted.

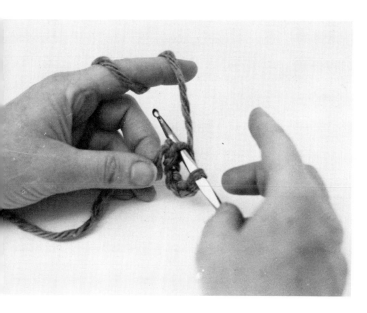

Begin a circle with a chain of 5 stitches and slip-stitch the chain together.

Crochet twice into each stitch as you go around the circle. Keep increasing in succeeding rounds, but less frequently. A good pattern is to increase every other stitch in the second row and every third stitch in the third row. If you are making a large circle, crochet one row without any increases between each row of increases, after the first three or four rounds.

Inserting Hard Objects into Crochet Circles

Mirrors, ceramic and metal discs, are just some of the types of hard objects which can be encased in crochet circles, adding sparkle and design interest to work being created.

To insert a hard object, make a circle large enough to fit the back of the object, then decrease so that the edge forms a holding frame as shown in this photo of a mirror being encased in metallic yarns. It is always best to use nonstretchy fibers when encasing objects in this manner.

A crocheted mirror necklace. Silver lamé thread and silver velour yarn have been combined. The inside of the velour is edged with lamé and some chains are worked back and forth at random for a spider-web effect, which is reflected in the mirror. The neckband is a velour yarn crochet band with lamé wrapping.

Another soft-hard crochet necklace. A driftwood disc with pen-and-ink features is encased in brown cotton. Picot stitches, made by chaining 3 to 5 stitches and then crocheting into the space right next to the chain, are made all around the edge to give a curly-hair effect. Beige lamé and novelty fibers are braided into a neck strand.

Hard-Soft Round Shapes

To give body and shape to crocheted rounds, ready-made rings or rings formed from hardware-store wire can be covered with single crochet stitches. The wire-based shapes can be built up with one or two rows of crochet stitches or expanded with the addition of ruffles formed by making lots of increases all around the circle. Separate crochet-covered shapes can be strung together to make ornaments such as the belt made by Marton Ackerman or the more elaborate adornments of Nancy Lipe. Shown later.

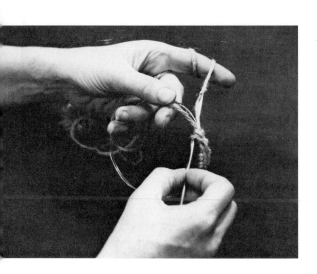

Hardware-store wire can be twisted into a ring of the desired size, and single crochet stitches can be worked all around as shown.

ROUND BEADS

Rounds can be worked into beads and stuffed for firmness. The round should be started with a chain of just 3 stitches and increased to the desired width. One or two rows can then be worked straight, which will cause the circle to cup. To close the bead, the procedure is reversed, decreasing all around until a closing point is reached. Stuffing should be inserted before the decreases are begun. These beads have many uses as buttons, ornaments, and so forth.

Beads can also be used as closing weights (as in Marton Ackerman's belts), as buttons, or in various stringing arrangements.

Nineteen 1½" brass rings were covered with crochet using shiny synthetic straw yarn and assembled into a handsome waist adornment. Marton Ackerman.

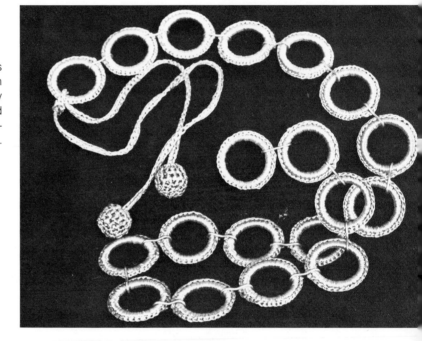

Crochet Bead Necklace with Ikat-Dyed Cotton

Since the materials used for crochet have had an enormous impact on what resulted, many crocheters dye at least some of their own yarns. We felt readers might be interested in a very old form of tie dyeing just starting to reengage the interest of contemporary fiber artists. In the more familiar tie-dye process, ready-woven fabric is dipped in dye, with the areas intended to remain uncolored being tied or stitched into circles or folds that will resist the dye. In ikat dyeing the yarn itself is tie dyed. We experimented with ikat by dyeing white cotton with blue household dye to obtain a blue-and-white delft effect. The finished yarn will offer different looks with different crafts. Wrapping, weaving, embroidery, knotting, and knotless netting could be done with ikat-dyed yarns. Cindy Fornari (whose work is shown in Chapter 7), while not actually using ikat-dyed yarn, was inspired by this method for her own painted-warp technique.

Cotton yarn is wound around T-pins pushed into pressboard. Sections are tied off at intervals with lengths of cotton.

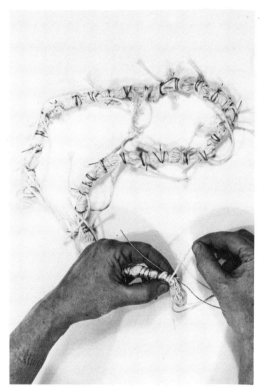

To avoid the need to make and cut open knots, pieces of wire are twisted around the tied cord. This makes the tying and untying both go very fast.

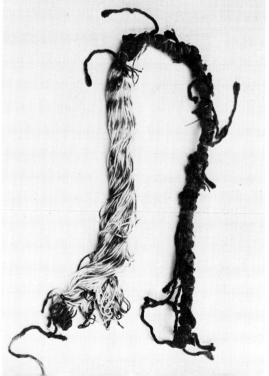

The yarn is dipped into hot household dye. When the wires are removed the tie-dyed or ikat pattern emerges.

An ikat-dyed necklace with stuffed, crocheted beads. The chain dangles were tied into the neckband of raffia cord wrapped with the ikat-dyed yarn.

Crochet Sculptures to Wear

Nancy and Dewey Lipe are both professional fiber artists. They work in partnership on nonwearable sculptures. The body pieces shown here are designed by Nancy, though Dewey often lends a helping hand with shaping the many metal rings Nancy uses to support and build her beautiful forms.

Nancy uses a variety of fibers from fine DMC cottons to cloud-soft thick yarns, many of which she dyes herself. To lend additional contrast, she makes her own fiber beads by wrapping sewing thread around foam and then stretching velour, velvet, or velveteen over this core. Touches of knotless netting (for details see Chapter 7) provide further textural interest. (Photographs, Dewey Lipe.)

Nancy Lipe at work with the many fibers she uses.

Dewey helps out in shaping some of the wire rings Nancy uses to build up the sculptural areas of her designs.

Once the neckline is worked out, the rest of the form is planned on a mannequin.

The mannequins have become a part of Nancy's work, acting not just as props but as integral parts of the finished piece when displayed. To achieve this unity between prop and neckpiece, Nancy sprays the mannequins (which she buys wherever she can find) with black paint. She covers the spray-painted form with single crochets worked in different directions to conform to body contours.

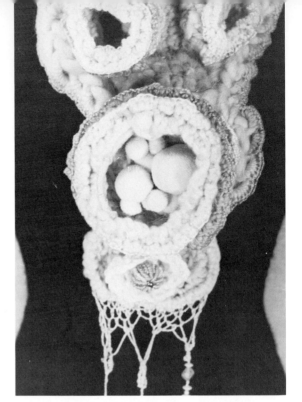

Detail of covered metal rings. Note that some areas are left open, whereas others are filled with the velvety puffs.

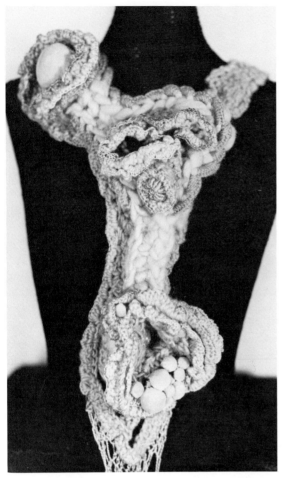

The completed body adornment. The velvet beads are foam-rubber wrapped with sewing thread and covered with fabric. The colors are very soft, delicate pinks. (See color section.)

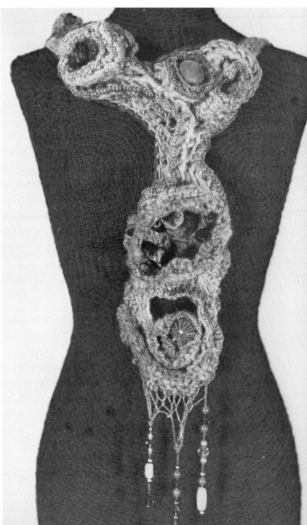

Another sculptural neckpiece with knotless-netting details.

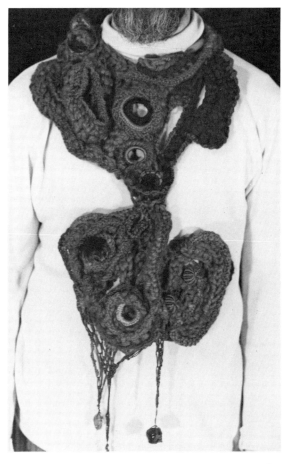

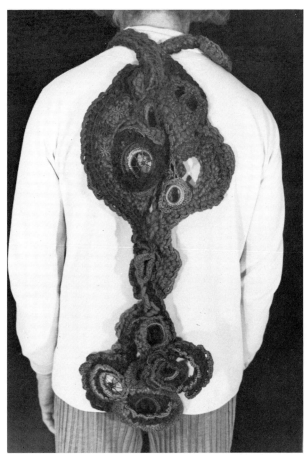

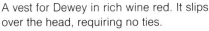
A vest for Dewey in rich wine red. It slips over the head, requiring no ties.

Rear view of Dewey's vest.

Hat Sculptures

A crocheted circle can be the beginning of a hat and a crocheted hat can be a simple functional covering or a fanciful adornment. Diana Willner's hats combined the best of everything. She uses beautiful wearable yarns and crochet forms that are comfortable and warm to wear. She blends yarns and colors with the skill of a painter and adds marvelous ruffles, all of which make up a piece that is a hat as well as a sculpture.

Like Nancy Lipe, Diana wanted a distinctive display form for her hats. She found stuffed and stitched muslin heads detailed with felt-tip pens an easy and amusing solution. She uses about a yard of muslin per head. A profile is drawn with exaggerated features to allow for the loss of surface space in the stuffing process. After the head is stitched and stuffed with polyester or foam, a ½'' dowel is inserted into the neck space. This dowel fits into a ½'' hole drilled into an 8-by-8-inch wooden base. These mannequin bases give Diana's hats a second life as sculptures when not worn. Crocheters who are strictly ''plain hat'' types can enjoy making the more fanciful kinds of hats and use them just as sculptures.

Crocheted hat with handmade base. Diana Willner.

Front and side view of Diana Willner's humorous bases.

Close-up of hat and mannequin profile.

Elizabeth Tuttle used the shape of the human head to crochet a wearable atlas. Soft blues, yellow, touches of green, and lavender make up the geography lesson.

Crochet Clothing:
Free Form and Three Dimensional

Crochet clothing can be created like a painting, with designs worked from the center out. The design can be planned carefully or allowed to develop as the work progresses. A garment must of course fit, but this is easily achieved without the restrictive up-and-down progression typical of most patterns. By copying the pieces of dressmaking patterns onto sheets of newsprint, the work can be held against these outlines for proper shaping, and ideas may be sketched in.

In the picture series that follows, the paper patterns have been numbered to show the order in which the design progressed. The jacket started with the idea for incorporating a weaving pattern into a crochet design. Filet crochet, a pattern of spacing stitches rather than a stitch in itself, seemed the ideal way to accomplish this. The collar and sleeves were designed after the front and back were well under way. By then it was clear that the woven areas should be repeated as a long cuff, but something more three dimensional was needed to accent the weave. The idea of the crocheted fur stemmed from the predominant yarn color used, a heathery beige which reminded us of the once popular beige Persian lamb coats. (See color section.)

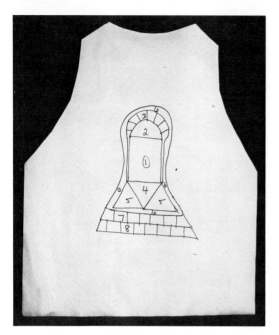

The central motif was the only part of the design sketched onto the paper pattern. The numbers show the order in which the design progressed. The checkered areas (3, 7, 8) indicate the areas of the filet weaving.

Filet crochet is not a stitch but a pattern. The patterns can be regular or irregular. For purposes of our ''weaving,'' the even pattern shown here seemed ideal. This pattern is created by making a double crochet stitch, then two chains, followed by two skipped chains. Another double crochet begins the next filet mesh. Larger spaces for wider strips could be made by making a treble crochet and leaving 3 spaces.

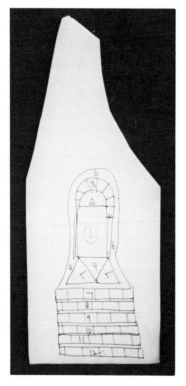

The central shapes and weaving pattern of the back were extended to the front of the jacket thus combining free-form crochet with a symmetrical design.

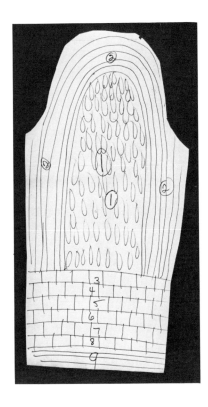

To unify the sleeve and the rest of the jacket, a long cuff with six rows of woven filet crochet was planned. The furry picot stitch was made only for the center portion of the sleeve to avoid bulk. The pattern is numbered to show the progression of the sleeve: 1) The picot fur area, 2) Single-crochet stitches worked back and forth around the fur center, 3) Six rows of filet mesh with woven crochet strips (numbers 3 through 8), and 4) Several rows of single crochets as an edging (number 9 on pattern).

To make the picot fur, a row of double crochet was alternated with a row of very long picot stitches made by chaining nine stitches and then single crocheting into the same space as the chain. By alternating rows of double crochets with rows of long picots, all the ''fur'' falls to the front of the fabric.

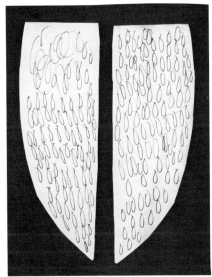

The fur collar seemed an obvious must. This was worked to fit two pattern pieces which, when sewn together, form a shawl collar.

Rear view of the finished jacket.

Front view of the jacket. The buttons are slabs of weathered wood sliced on a saw, buffed, and drilled for sewing.

Close-up view of the jacket.

The Details That Count:
Buttons and Linings

When creating clothing that doubles as art as well as a body covering, every detail is worth special effort. Interesting beads, wrappings (see pages 104 and 105), and weathered wood are some of the ways unusual closings can be made. Weathered-wood buttons are especially useful, since they lend themselves to use as necklaces as well as buttons. This kind of wood is easily found, and though the photographs show the buttons being made with electric tools, the wood is soft enough to be easily sliced with a handsaw and shaped with an ordinary piece of sandpaper.

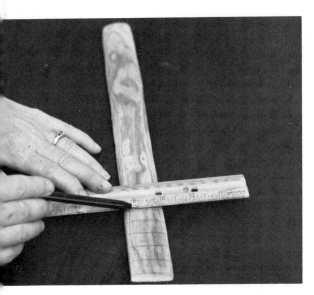

To make wooden beads, select a slab of weathered wood approximately ¼-inch thick, and mark for slicing.

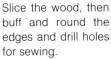

Slice the wood, then buff and round the edges and drill holes for sewing.

To give a crocheted jacket the warmth and "hang" of a coat, a lining is important. We used a lining of soft wool, cut to fit the paper pattern and hand printed with designs shaped out of plastelene. (See instructions for this printing method in Chapter 2.) The signature at the lower right was made with two small printers, one for *el* and another for *yse.*

The weaving technique is effective for necklaces, as are the driftwood buttons, this time rounded and etched with a woodburning tool. The driftwood is held in place by working stitches right off the surface of the necklace, going in a circle and then decreasing sharply so the edges hold the wood in place. Gold lamé thread and coral beads are used as an edging.

A completely different weaving effect results when single crochet strips are used for both warp and weft. This vest is a wearable adaptation of a blanket by Helen Bitar. Those wishing to experiment with this technique are advised to make lots of strips in different colors, to be able to play with the design. This method is far more time consuming than filet-mesh weaving.

The jacket and vest just shown are worked in a symmetrical pattern. Crochet lends itself to completely asymmetrical methods, as illustrated by this crazy-quilt vest, also sized against a paper pattern.

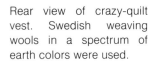

Rear view of crazy-quilt vest. Swedish weaving wools in a spectrum of earth colors were used.

More Crocheted Body Art

Fancy pants, gloves, and mittens are just a few more ideas for body ornamentation with crochet.

An assemblage of crocheted shapes, this lovely collar was made with hand-spun and hand-dyed yarns. Sheila Klein. Photo courtesy artist.

These wonderful, clingy pants were crocheted all in red. Roblee Fulton. Photo courtesy artist.

Variegated wool in shades of yellow, orange, and brown, and bits of leather combined cleverly to make these aptly titled Tiger Gloves. Elizabeth Tuttle. Photo courtesy artist.

Another catchy idea crocheted with variegated wool, plus a touch of leather. O Basketball Slippers. Elizabeth Tuttle. Photo courtesy artist.

Knitted and Crocheted Body Art

Although knitting, in spite of its continued popularity as a practical and relaxing hobby, has not stimulated quite the degree of excitement and artistic innovation as crochet, a number of artists have successfully incorporated knitting and crochet. These stunning pieces will perhaps inspire others to experiment with marrying the two crafts.

Sheila Klein's knitted and crocheted Off-Hours Knight is a magnificent interpretation of a historic costume. The artist used silvery gray for the side panels, and creamy off-white with deep, almost rust red for the edges. Photo courtesy artist.

Norma Minkowitz's work is incomparable. Her tiny crocheted figures have become a sort of trademark. Many of her admirers marvel not only at the intricacy and excellence of her craftsmanship but at her ability constantly to make fresh and exciting statements with the familiar little figures. This wonderful cloak is a stunning case in point: Ninety—yes, ninety—figures have been appliquéd to the yoke.

Close-up of the yoke.

Rear view of the cloak.

For those who feel that art garments are strictly for the very young, very tall, or very slim, here is Norma Minkowitz with her first crochet teacher, her mother, Fania Chigrinsky. The crocheted and knitted pieces worn by mother and daughter look strikingly beautiful without being the least "far out." Photo, Bob Hanson.

Crochet Flowers

The ease with which ruffles and shapes can be crocheted makes flowers a most appealing undertaking. They can be large and fantastic, or tiny accents to incorporate into a garment. They are useful as pin-ons or appliqués for clothing, hats, collars, belts, and so forth. Yarns and colors can be chosen for realistic or fantastic flowers. (For other flower-making methods refer to the Index.)

A crocheted beret lent to us by Ahuvah Bebe Dushey is appliquéd with three kinds of crochet flowers—a ruffled fantasy flower at the top, a lilac at bottom left, and a sunflower at the lower right.

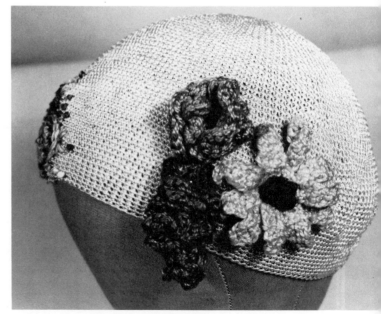

Ruffled Fantasy Flower

Start with a chain of 3 stitches and slip-stitch to make a circle. Keep crocheting around the circle. Go three and four times into each stitch to create the ruffles. When making larger flowers, edge the ruffles with contrasting yarns.

Lilacs

The lilac shown on Ahuvah Bebe Dushey's hat was made in thick handspun yarn. The lilac started with a chain of 3, slip-stitched into a circle. The circle was increased until the flower had the desired fullness for the top. The single crochet stitch with picots (a chain of three and back into the same space as the chain) was used. The shape continued in a tube, decreasing all around and eventually closing the tube at the bottom or point of the flower. Tiny green triangles were crocheted to the top by chaining on three stitches and working back and forth once, then decreasing on each side.

Sunflowers

The sunflower on the hat is made with mercerized cotton. A small center circle is made from dark gold cotton. Long triangle shapes are added all around for the leaves. Each leaf is started with three stitches, with a few increases made. The ends of the leaves are brought to a point with sharp decreases. Some of the leaves are worked on top of other leaves to make a nice full flower. To "vein" the leaves and avoid the necessity of starting each leaf with new yarn, a row of single crochets is worked back along the center of the leaf. This brings you back to the base of the leaf, ready to begin a new one without breaking off the yarn.

Here is the sunflower appliquéd to the upper portion of the sleeve of a crocheted jacket. (See page 106 for a front close-up view).

Hydrangeas

Still another ruffly flower, similar to the lilac shown on the hat, can be made in a crochet variation of the patchwork Yo-Yo.

Blue mercerized cotton is crocheted into a 3-to-4-inch-diameter circle. Picot ruffles are worked onto the surface of one side of the circle (turned under in photo), making for a very firm fabric.

The circle is basted and the basting thread pulled tight so that the shape is gathered into a ball.

The hydrangea!

The giant, ruffled flower on this hat by Nancy Lipe could be used as an independent accent, in its full size or smaller.

7

NETTED AND WOVEN FABRICS

This chapter is a continuation of the off-loom weaving techniques described in the two previous ones. Wrapping and coiling, as well as crochet, combine beautifully with knotless netting and weaving. The idea here, as throughout this book, is to sample everything presented as one would a smorgasbord and then choose one's favorites to use and study in detail.

Knotless Netting

Knotless netting is historically associated with lace making. It has been used for countless years by Ecuadorians to make bags and by Alaskan Indians to make fishing nets.

This technique is not as well known as crochet, weaving, or macramé among contemporary fiber enthusiasts. However, as more and more artists are discovering its versatility, this very easy and relaxing method of looping stitches with a needle is likely to gain more and more favor as an exciting new-old craft.

An ancient knotless-netting container from Ecuador. From the collection of Maggie Brosnan. Photo courtesy artist.

The creation of soft jewelry provides an excellent opportunity to try knotless netting, either by itself or in combination with crochet or weaving. The delicate look of the loops against a thick and nubby woven or crocheted fabric is almost magical. For items receiving wear and tear, the loops can be pulled very tight so that a solid fabric is created.

The netting or looping can be started from a straight holding cord like macramé or from a circular one. We felt the latter offered the most immediate and diverse application to the soft jeweler, so we asked Nancy Lipe to create a teaching demonstration using a round holding cord. Nancy's simple and attractive necklace clearly illustrates not just the steps for knotless netting, but its worth as an independent or adjunct soft-jewelry technique.

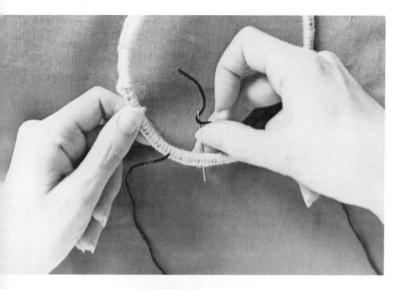

A necklace cord has been covered with buttonhole stitches.
Single crochet stitches could be
worked around the cord also.
The netting cord (DMC pearl
cotton, size 3) has been
threaded onto a needle and is
started from left to right.

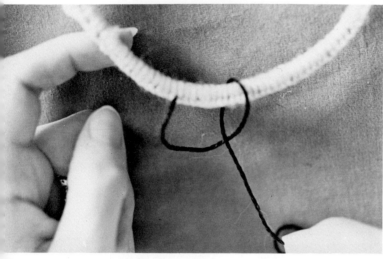

Loops are made as shown.
Nancy works on a flat foam-
rubber cushion onto which a
quilted mattress pad has been
draped. This enables her to pin
down her work as it progresses,
though at this beginning stage
she likes her work to be free for
handling.

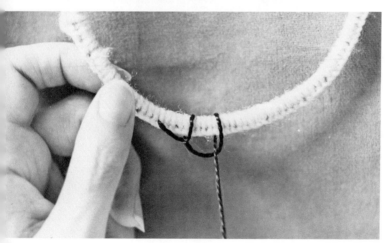

The loops continue from left to
right.

When the end of a row is reached, Nancy makes a holding knot. This is not a must, but it helps to stabilize the edges of the work and also offers a solution for tying off and weaving in loose ends.

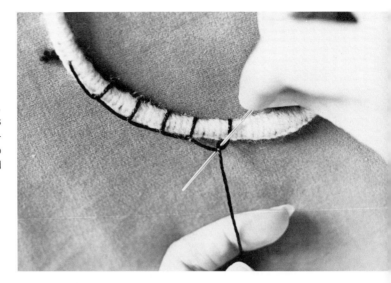

The holding knot is tightened.

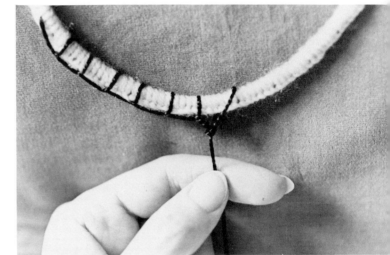

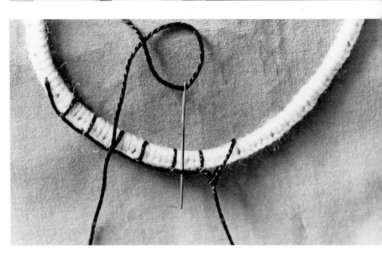

The looping continues . . .

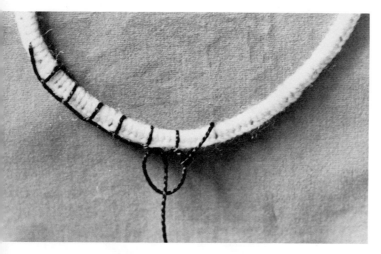

. . . this time going from right to left.

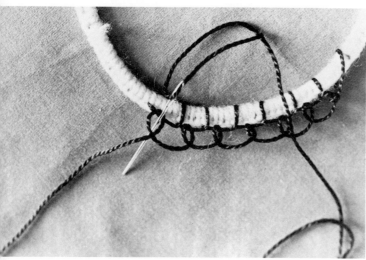

A holding knot is made at the other end before turning to go back from left to right, and so on.

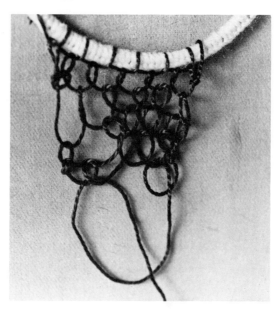

To create open areas or holes, make a large loop as shown.

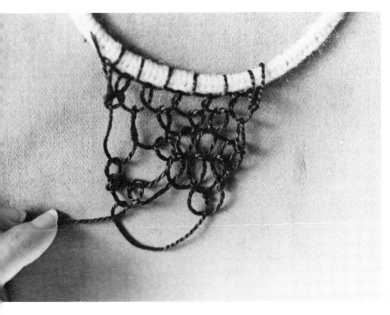

Then pull it up so that a space as big or as small as you want is created.

Here is a row worked back over the hole made in the previous hole.

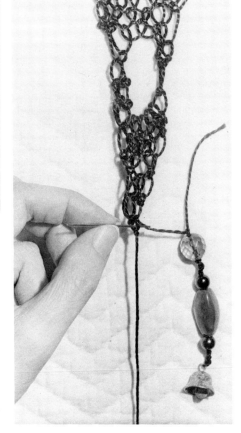

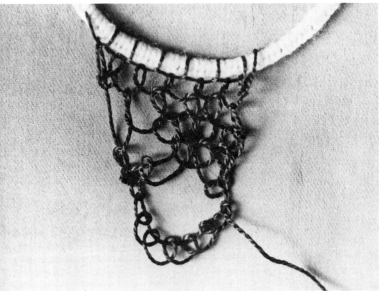

To narrow down the necklace or decrease, skip some loops. Usually the end loops are skipped, but this can vary with the shape wanted. The necklace illustrated is brought to a point and ended with a holding knot to which beads will be tied.

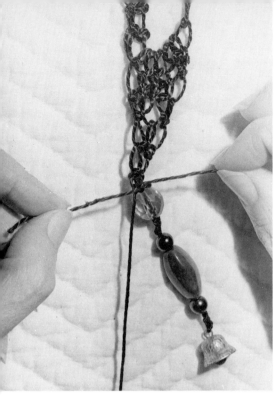

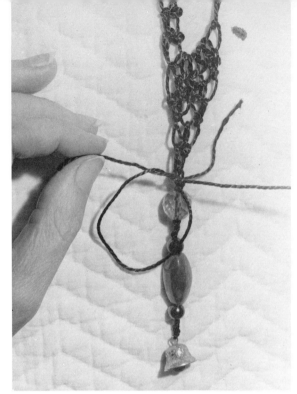

The ends of the strung beads are tied . . .

. . . and tied again.

The finished necklace. The holding cord has been covered with a cotton-and-rayon-blend yarn and more beads.

Knotless Netting Variations

Variations in pattern as well as shape can be made by inserting the needle several times into each loop. To narrow down the shape or to decrease it, loops can be skipped.

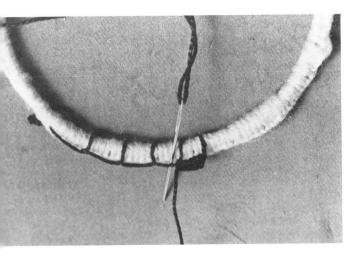

Contrasts can be created by inserting the needle several times into each loop.

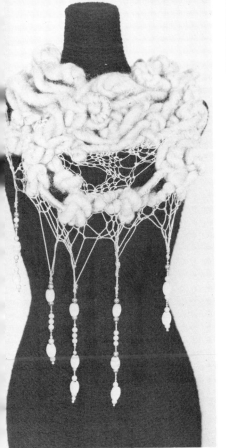

Here we see another necklace started with rows of single loops followed by a pattern of many stitches into one loop.

An ethereally beautiful body piece of fleecy crochet with areas of knotless netting. Nancy Lipe. Photo, Dewey Lipe.

Creating Tight Weaves and Cupped Shapes

Yvonne Porcella works her knotless netting very firmly and tightly in the manner of Ecuadorian bag makers. She uses all kinds of yarns, sometimes so thick that they won't go through a needle but must be taped so that the tip of the taped yarn is used as a needle. Yvonne likes to make both flat and three-dimensional circular shapes. (Photographs, Dick Milligan.)

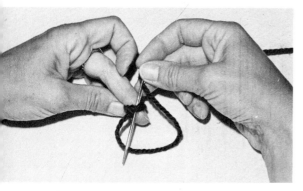

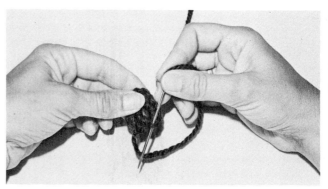

Yvonne Porcella usually starts her cup shapes by winding yarn over her fingers. Photo, Dick Milligan.

To create a cupped or three-dimensional shape, she decreases her loops after the first two rows. Photo, Dick Milligan.

Here are a variety of circular shapes. At the top, two cupped shapes; at bottom left, an old window-shade pull covered with knotless netting; at lower right, a circular shape opened out into one direction. Photo, Dick Milligan.

This flowerlike ornament, which could be appliquéd to a garment, like some of the other flower ideas presented throughout this book (see Index), combines numerous yarns and shapes. Photo, Dick Milligan.

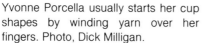

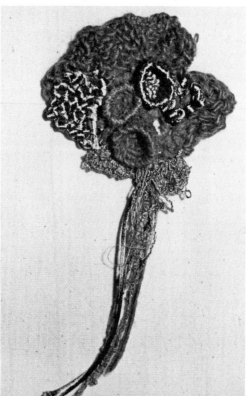

This handsome bag by Linda Witt shows the wonderful interaction of colors possible with knotless netting. The purse closes with a yarn-wound spool. Photo, Maggie Brosnan.

Knotless-netted collar necklace made by Judy Smaha. Wrapped fibers are interlaced through the netting. Photo, Maggie Brosnan.

Close-up of the petal details of Jan Alderson's necklace.

Jan Alderson backs her knotless netting with chamois leather. Photo, Maggie Brosnan.

Wearable Weaving

To the uninitiated, weaving might seem like a formidable craft to undertake. The thought of looms and shuttles can intimidate one from a standpoint of expense as well as the difficulty of mastering the technique. Yet, while weaving is indeed a serious craft to which students can and do devote years of study, wonderful results can be achieved easily with simple handmade devices onto which the warp thread, which constitutes the basis of all weaving, is stretched. For those who wish to weave shaped forms such as garments or jewelry, handmade devices offer many advantages over conventional looms, since the loom can be constructed specifically with the end result in mind. In the following pages you will see some of the devices and creations made by innovative weavers. Other ideas are limited only by one's imagination.

Notched Cardboard Loom Bib Collar

The following demonstration illustrates the use of the cardboard loom. This type of weaving is fast and relaxing, with the possibility for beautiful and very wearable results.

Here are the materials to be used: Cardboard to be notched at each end for winding the warp yarn, yarns, a needle for carrying the weft or cross yarns over and under the warp thread, a comb for pushing the weft yarns close together (in weaver's language this is called beating the weft), scissors, and beads for decorative details.

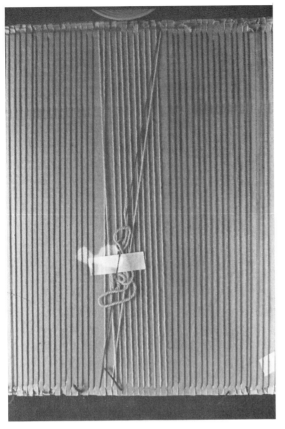

The yarn is warped around the notches, carried from front to back, and attached with masking tape as shown.

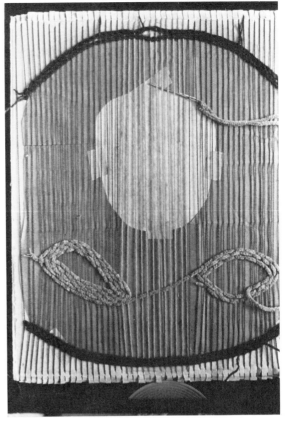

A paper pattern for the neckline opening is taped underneath the warp threads of the front on the loom and the needle weaving is begun. The color patterns can be sketched out and placed in back of the warp, or worked free form as shown. The weaving can begin anywhere.

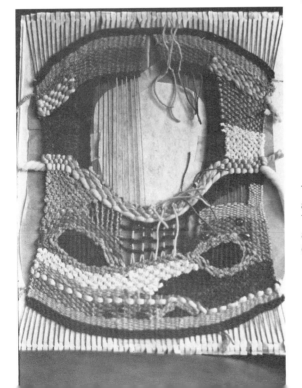

The completed weaving is cut, two threads at a time. The loose ends are knotted together. To avoid this step, the loom can be warped around the points so that only the front of the cardboard is covered with warp threads.

A row of chain stitches was made along the warp edges and beaded fringes were added for a decorative effect. (See color section.)

Rear view of the collar. The slit opening enables the wearer to slip the piece over the head.

Pinned Loom Collar

Warp threads can also be attached to the loom by means of pins instead of notches.

Yvonne Porcella has positioned a warping pattern for a large collar into a pressboard. A carrier cord (to fit the circle of the neck) is pinned to the top of the warp and warp threads, a pair at a time, are put onto this carrier with a lark's-head knot, as for beginning macramé (see page 178). Photos, courtesy artist.

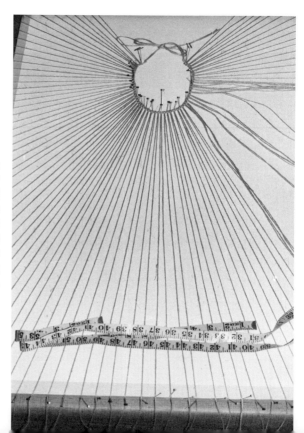

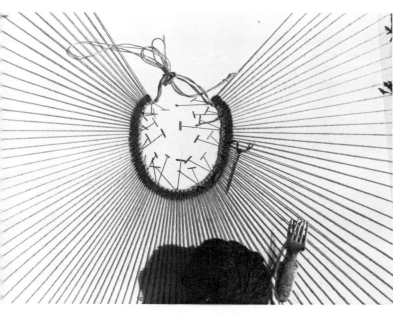

The weaving is begun.

The finished collar was made expressly to display the pre-Columbian spindle beads.

Rear view of the collar.

Garments Woven on a One-Piece Loom

An entire garment can be made in one piece by drawing the outline of the garment onto a piece of cardboard folded in half, notching the warping points, and then needle weaving the front and back of the loom. Mary Lou Higgins uses this method for beginners' workshops, and her students are invariably thrilled with the idea of making a complete garment so fast and so easily. The following demonstration is done with a miniature cardboard model for ease of handling. Readers might just try out this technique for a doll-sized garment first.

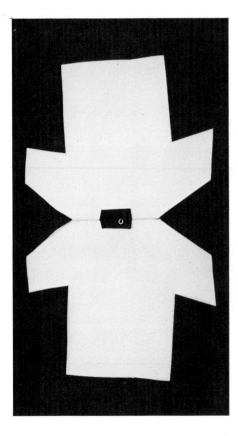

The outline of the garment is drawn onto cardboard which has been folded in half, then cut and notched as shown.

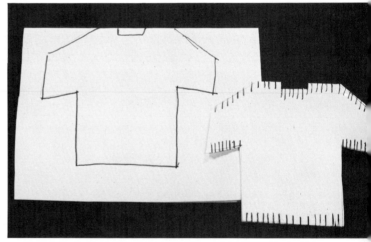

Here is what has actually been cut out, shown only for demonstration purposes. In actual use, the cardboard *must be kept closed* and notched as if it were one single piece.

The left front and sleeve of the jacket are needle woven at random, with some beads added. By weaving only to the center of the front, a natural opening will be created.

This tapestry-woven jacket could have been made on a cardboard loom, though once weavers get into the intricacies of tapestry weaving and become master weavers like Bucky King, who made this jacket, they usually do switch to the faster-moving shuttle looms.

Nailed Frame Looms

Nails evenly spaced at either end of a wooden frame allow for an easy warp-threading procedure. The openness of the frame permits the weaving to proceed freely.

The top of a woven apron removed from its nail loom. Madge Copeland. Photos courtesy artist.

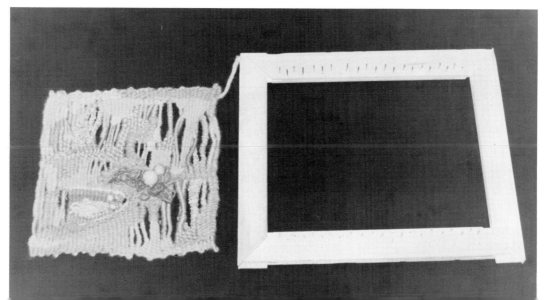

The bib of the apron is fringed with straps woven on a large loom.

Another nail-loomed apron, this one with a closely wrapped weaving pattern for the bib and partially wrapped fringes for the skirt. Yvonne Porcella.

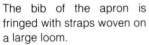

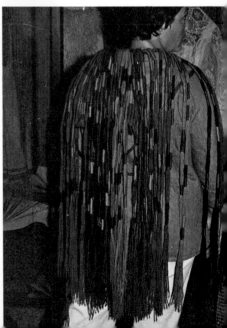

The apron can also be worn as a shoulder cape. Photo, Dick Milligan.

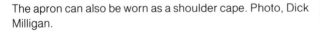

Woven body bag.   Here is the loom on which it was woven. Yvonne
Porcella.

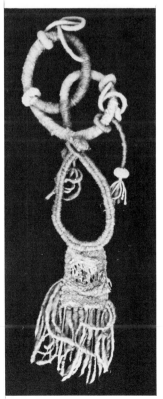

Cardboard-loom-woven bib. Some
weft threads were allowed to remain
loose and were later wrapped with
feathers and silk. A little pocket attached to the back makes this a very
functional necklace. Joan Schulze.

Wrapped necklace with a
cardboard-loom-woven pen-
dant. Madge Copeland.

Other People's Weaving—Recycled

Nothing is accidentproof. A woven pillow suffered the ravages of a cigarette burn. A square of the weaving which remained in good condition was edged with single crochet. Fringes were made at the bottom and secured with beads.

Crochet is added to woven edge.

A neck chain was crocheted and a little mad-money pocket was sewn to the back, giving new life to an old weaving.

Stick Weaving

Alice Babcock creates delicate hair combs by wrapping yarn on sanded and polished dowels. The yarn is woven over and under the sticks as shown.

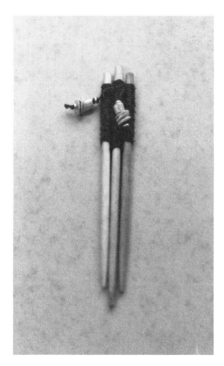

Beads are secured into the closing.

Susan Green uses the stick-weaving technique to fashion a highly sophisticated necklace of waxed linen and snail shells. The wrapped cords at the bottom of the necklace provide the center structure for the over-and-under stick weaving. Photo, Almut Helmann.

Painted Loom Weaving

Cindy Fornari's inspiration for what she describes as painted loom weaving is the ikat technique of tie-dyeing yarns (see Chapter 6). Instead of dyeing her yarns before warping the loom, Cindy actually applies the dyes directly to the warp. When the weft threads are woven through the painted warp, a broken-color design results. Cindy uses a cotton warp and emphasizes the broken-color effect with a thick-and-thin novelty cotton weft. For those interested in trying this method of weaving, a professional loom is not necessary. Any of the simple looms already described would work. And dyes, including acrylic paints thinned with water, may be used, though Cindy recommends direct dyes, since they are made to be painted directly on fabric with simple fixing methods. Light-colored warps are best. (Most of Cindy's weavings are in very soft muted colors on off-white backgrounds.) Put a piece of paper under the warp to prevent dye from dripping on the floor or the bottom of the loom. (Photographs, Dan Fornari.)

Cindy Fornari applies a butterfly design to her warp, using a watercolor brush for the dyes.

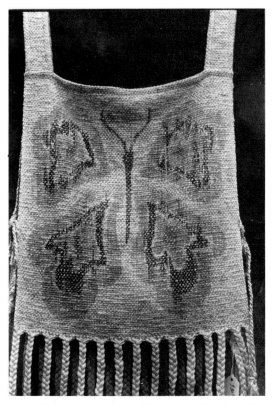

The broken-color effect created when the weft is woven through the painted warp gives the butterfly design of this simply shaped bib subtlety. The fringed ends are braided.

Another painted-warp garment. The construction of the tunic is a simple rectangle, shaped to conform to the body with side ties.

Woven Wearables on a Large Scale—Inspirations

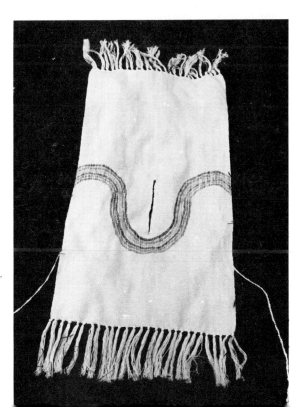

Construction of the tunic.

Mary Lou Higgins's true love in weaving is the double weave, shown at its best in this portrait coat the artist entitled Reversible Faces. Photo, Edward Higgins.

Fur can be woven right into a garment. The beauty of this technique is that it enables the weaver to use end pieces of expensive fur at low cost, since they are of little or no use to furriers. This coat of Acrilan and lynch fur was woven by Mary Lou Higgins and is owned by jeweler Wendy Ramshaw. Photo, Edward Higgins.

The drama inherent in handwoven garments is strikingly evident in this Penguin Coat by Louise Todd Cope.

Strips of weaving can be combined to achieve rhythm and motion in a design, as, for example, in Louise Todd Cope's River Dress.

A merger of weaving and knotless netting by Bucky King. This is the rear view of a blouse.

8

LEATHER, MACRAMÉ, AND FEATHERS

The soft and supple qualities of leather invite and inspire the designer of body coverings. The cheapest, most lightweight scraps, often considered throwaways, are frequently the best for this purpose. They can be stitched, painted, and appliquéd like other fabrics, with the texture of the leather adding its own sensuous stamp of uniqueness. The ideas presented in this chapter can be supplemented with those found in Chapters 2 and 3, most of which lend themselves to construction in leather.

The sailor's ancient art of macramé has enjoyed such a strong surge of interest that too many poorly thought out and imitative knotted items have threatened to relegate the craft to the status of a passing fad. Fortunately, much good design has outweighed the fad items, and macramé remains alive and well as a useful and artistic fiber craft.

Both macramé and feathers have a natural affinity with leather. We show them here used both independently and in combination with leather.

Tie-Dyed Chamois

To prove that leather can be an economical material lending itself to a multitude of decorative methods, we begin with an imaginative necklet made by Gayle Feller with grocery-store chamois. The artist tied and dyed the chamois and cut a hole, which she filled in with needle weaving. This weaving is echoed at the closing neckband.

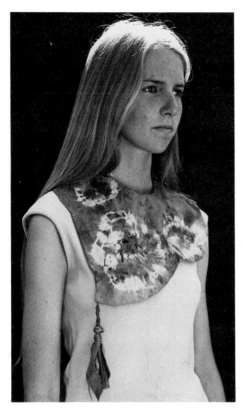

Tie-dyed chamois necklet with inserts of needle weaving.

Needle weaving is carried through at the neckline.

A ceramic bead was glazed to coincide with the colors of the tie-dyed chamois.

Chamois and Fabric Hanging Bag

Using chamois once again, Gayle Feller creates an amusing little bag to be hung on the wall as a manicure equipment holder or worn on a belt as a handy conversation piece. She utilizes chamois for the ''skin'' of the hand. The fingers are decorated with a real ring. The nails are painted pink, and the lines around nails and knuckles are etched with a woodburning tool. A tapestry shirt cuff complements the purple leather cuff.

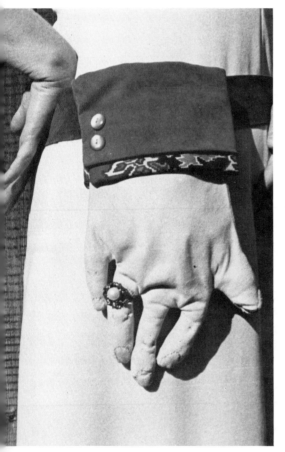

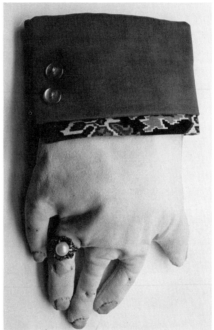

Chamois and fabric belt bag.

It can be used as a wall hanging.

The cuff is lifted to reveal a tattoo etched with a woodburning tool.

Another talented leathercrafter, Tina Johnson, shows her Jewel Thieves' Hat and Gloves. It began with a pair of cotton work gloves which the artist used as a pattern after removing the stitching. Notice the pouch on the hat. Photo, Brian E. Rybolt.

Painted and Appliquéd Leather

John Miles's adventure with leather began when he discovered that people were actually throwing away the colorful, lightweight leathers which now serve as the raw materials for his painterly garments. Call it thrift or a sense for ecology, but John felt compelled to do something with the leather he saw so casually discarded. He taught himself to use a sewing machine and began to sew basically simple clothes, ornamented with patchwork and appliqué.

John Miles's workroom requires no special outfitting, since his chief equipment is the sewing machine. The leathers he works with are so light that a regular home sewing machine is adequate.

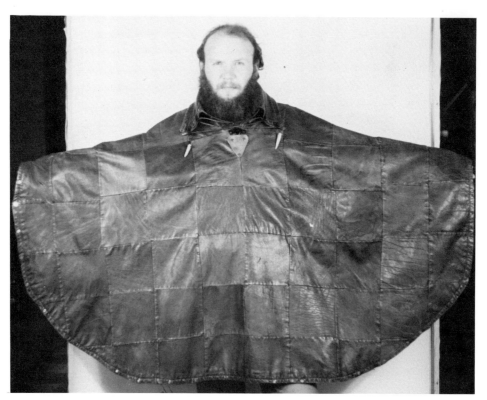

John poses in a striking patchwork cape reminiscent of the chasubles worn by old-time ecclesiastics. The leathers are lightweight soft brown; a lining of fur lends warmth.

This simple, loosely fitted style is one of the artist's favorites. All the appliqués are machine stitched.

A stunning collaborative effort. The painting was done by Art Ellis and Kim Gerney. Painting and appliqués were carefully correlated. (See color section.)

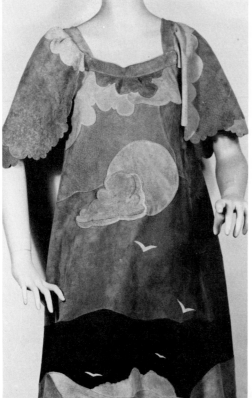

Some soft leathers are cool and weather-resistant enough to serve for active sportswear. This appliquéd leather bikini really *does* get wet.

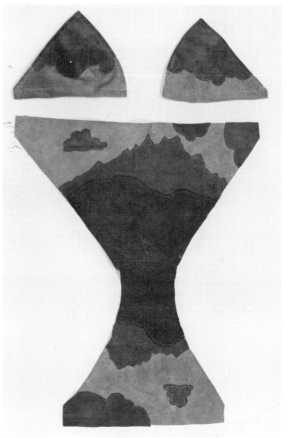

The construction of the bikini is simple. Tie closings make the size adjustable.

California designer-artist Colette uses leather appliqué as a vehicle for breathtakingly beautiful wearable landscapes. Her Arizona Mountain Vest is reversible to solid-brown leather. Photo courtesy artist.

Molded Leather

Marcia Lloyd takes advantage of leather's pliability in the construction of truly unusual body bags, leather and silver jewelry, and flower pin-ons that can double as decorative room accessories. To mold or stamp leather, it must be thoroughly dampened and then stamped or impressed over a form. When the leather dries, the details of the mold are permanently embedded in the leather.

A rich patina-and-mold motif accentuates the appropriateness of a handbag to its wearer. The prop was designed by Tony Lloyd.

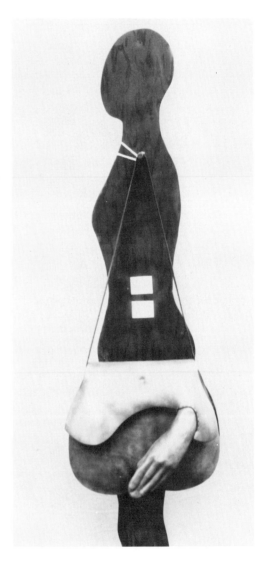

Leather and silver bracelet. Marcia Lloyd.

Most leather flowers we've seen lack distinction or pliability. Marcia Lloyd's roses are almost more beautiful than the real thing, thanks to her expert handling of materials and subtle use of dyes.

Marcia's flowers are as much at home in a vase as on a hat, another example of the duality of body adornments.

Macramé

Knotting, like crochet or knotless netting, need not involve mastery of all available techniques. The clove hitch and the square knot are sufficient for the creation of innovative body coverings. Whole garments can be knotted or just small areas of knotting utilized to more or less secure additional jewelry materials such as beads and feathers. Large areas of holding cord can be left unknotted, which not only makes things progress quite readily, but allows for negative design areas.

Sol Schwartz demonstrates the basics of knotting.

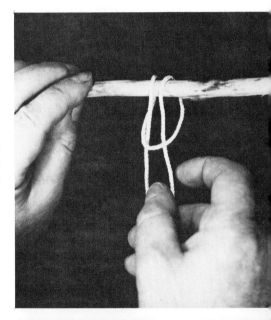

All macramé starts by folding a cord in half and looping it over a holding cord or stick as shown. When pulled tight, the holding or lark's-head knot is complete.

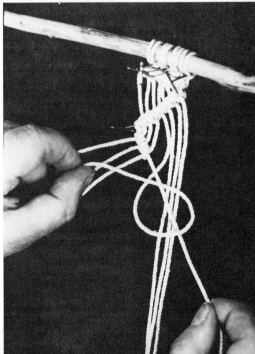

To make a clove hitch, loop and knot two cords as shown. Since this can be worked diagonally, vertically, or horizontally, the design applications are self-evident.

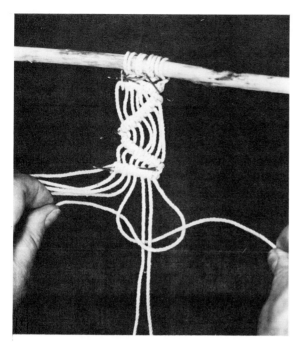

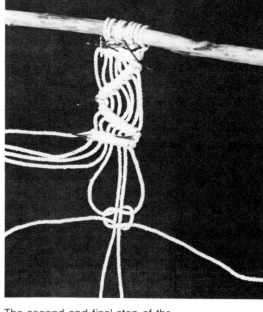

The square knot is made with four cords. The cord at the right of the two center cords is brought over and to the left. The cord at the left is brought under and to the right. This is the first step in a two-step procedure.

The second and final step of the square knot involves bringing the left cord over and to the right of the center cord and the right under and up through the loops formed by the left cord. When the loops are pulled tight, the square knot is complete.

Louise Todd Cope effectively interprets the basics of macramé square knotting plus wrapping—in jute and natural linen.

Diagonal clove hitches, sparingly used, show off a cowrie shell, clear champagne beads, and hackle feathers. Paul Johnson. Photo, Ken Korsh.

Tina Johnson's Saw-Tooth Fetish began at the back of the neck and was worked around a dress form. Linen and vegetable-dyed wools are used for wrapping and for horizontal and vertical clove hitches. Photo, Paul Boyer.

Another of Tina Johnson's organic necklaces in silver and macramé with natural materials. Photo, Paul Boyer.

Silver rattail knotted around an assortment of unusual beads, including empty cartridges, results in a sleek body covering.

For those searching for something new and different in macramé, Debbie Susswein may inspire them with a bib knotted from paper cord. It buttons at the back of the neck and across the back.

Francie Adams's aptly named Fertility Vest, with its shaggy, hairy quality evokes images of ritual chants and dances. It is constructed with knotted and woven sections. Photo, Roger Rosenblatt.

Since fiber necklaces are so much lighter than traditional metal jewelry, they often grow into jewelry garments like this macramé waistcoat by Mary Lou Higgins. Photo, Edward Higgins.

Macramé to Turn Plain Clothes into Fancy Ones

Dolly Curtis likes her clothes plain, with dramatic accents. She decided to make a macramé neckpiece an integral part of a dress.

Dolly Curtis knotted an all-in-one yoke onto a board.

The alternating-square-knot pattern in progress.

The yoke and dress modeled by its designer-owner.

Macramé and Crochet with Leather

With the aid of a hole punch, even the stiffest leathers can be combined with yarns and cords. Single crochet stitches can be worked right into the holes or into blanket stitches. Macramé holding knots can be made through the holes.

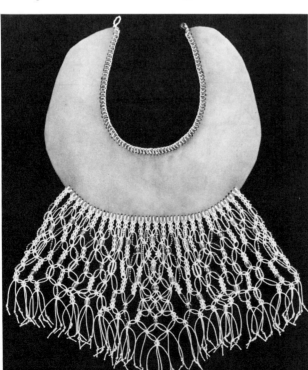

Macramé and beads worked off a hole-punched leather collar. Jean Tice.

Quilted and macramé leather neck bag. Tina Johnson. Photo, Brian E. Rybolt.

Holes of different sizes can be made along edges of leather pieces with the aid of a leather punch, and single crochet stitches can be worked right into the holes.

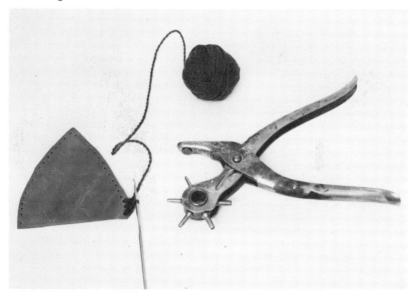

A network of single crochets worked from a hole-punched leather circle to fashion a hair ornament. The crossbar is a sanded and polished twig from a tree.

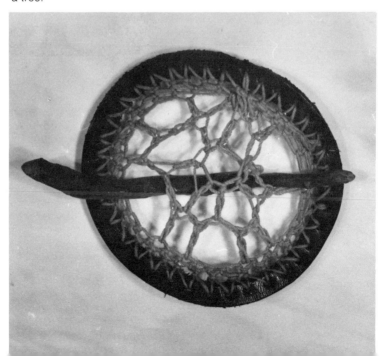

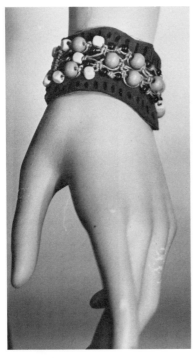

Macramé and beads appliqued to a suede bracelet. Jean Tice.

Macramé and beads, worked off the edge of a suede upper-arm bracelet. Jean Tice.

Feathers

Throughout the history of fashion and personal ornamentation, the sensuous elegance and almost limitless color palette of feathers have played distinctive roles. Many people in ancient cultures wore feather adornments not only for their beauty but for their religious symbolism as well. Although the use of some feathers from endangered species has been declared illegal, there are still plenty of lovely feathers available for those who want to use them creatively. The use of feathers from all food birds is all right, and those who don't live near chicken, turkey, or pheasant farms will find feather dealers throughout the country. (See Sources of Supplies.)

Nicki Marx, a California artist in feathers, whose body coverings have won her much-deserved recognition, admits that working with feathers can seem frustrating and seemingly impossible at first. "You get the feathers stuck in your fingers and it seems to take forever," Nicki told us. But she adds an encouraging note for those with determination: "After the first few attempts, and once you get to understand and work with the medium, it gets easier."

Nicki's basic working method consists of first making a template of paper or cardboard. The shape is then translated to leather with a scribing tool and cut out. Any white glue is next either spread on the leather backing or the base of each feather is dipped into the glue. The feathers are laid one on top of the other, each covering the end of the one before. As the feather is put down it is pressed into the glue so it will hold. (Photographs courtesy artist)

Nicki Marx working on a breastplate. She uses a Q-tip to facilitate the application of glue to leather and feathers.

The artist models a breastplate of ringneck pheasant and chicken feathers on leather. Photo, Glenn Moody.

Ringneck pheasant pendant with abalone shell.

Feather pendants and collar of ringneck pheasant, marabou turkey, and guinea hen feathers.

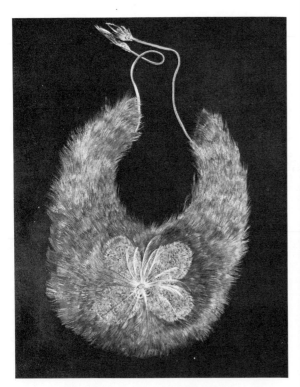

Stone and jade plus ringneck and golden pheasant feathers assembled into a breastplate entitled Shamrock.

A truly "feel beautiful" garment—marabou and turkey feathers on a fringed vest. Photo, Dave Milton.

Those who don't like to glue can wrap their feathers. The top of the wrapping warp can be looped so that the feathers can be combined with crochet, macramé, or weaving. Or the feathers can be wrapped right into a separately wrapped band in the manner of this necklace of beige, brown, and black linen with wrapped pheasant feathers. Susan Green. Photo, Almut Helmann.

Macramé and Feather Adornments

Paul Johnson's feather and macramé halters are assemblages of beads, bones, feathers, and macramé. His methods and materials are a radiant marriage between the mood of the primitive and the polish of Fabergé.

Black linen macramé accents a halter of boar tusks plus a fascinating assortment of fish scales, African bone beads, crystal and glass beads, a 79-carat smoke topaz quartz, and hackle and guinea hen feathers. It's chamois lined. Paul Johnson. Photo courtesy artist.

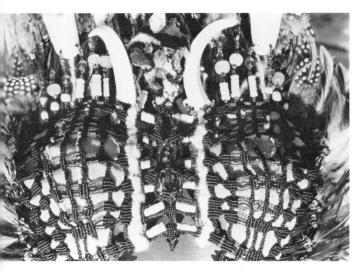

Detail of boar tusk halter.

Another tusk shell halter with chamois lining, waxed linen macramé, and assorted hackle and duck feathers. Paul Johnson. Photo courtesy artist.

Nancy Grossman's Black, though created not as a body adornment but as a strictly sculptural statement, nevertheless seems a fitting conclusion to this chapter. Photo by Eeva-Inkeri, courtesy Cordier & Ekstrom.

9

POTPOURRI OF METHODS AND IDEAS

Although the entire concept of this book is one defying rigid classification, there were some ideas which, though they might have been included elsewhere, seemed to demand a chapter of their own. None of these methods and tools are likely to be used to make body adornments on an extensive scale. Decoupage is primarily a paper craft, ideally suited to backgrounds other than fabric. Rug and latch hooking offer much more freedom of scope and design when done on a large scale. Yet there is stimulation and fun in adapting an essentially large-scale craft to a wearable dimension. For the gadget lover, devices like Doreen Sinnett's minihook and Eleanor Lofton's "hork" may spark ideas for other uses and possibly stir the reader's own talents for invention. The easy-zipper, wool-and-wire, and felt ideas should prove especially noteworthy for those in low-budget teaching situations.

Plastic-Covered, Felt-Encased Drawings

Barbara Kensler likes railroad board as a background for her delicate line drawings. She finds this a perfect weight for easy cutting and likes the many colors in which it is available. To protect her drawings, she covers her work with clear contact paper (she prefers a dull finish) and then inserts it into a felt frame. The use of felt simplifies the framing process, since the cut edge is the finished one. This technique could be adapted by watercolorists, paper collage artists, and others.

Pen-and-ink drawings on railroad board, encased in felt frames and assembled into a one-of-a-kind body ornament by Barbara Kensler.

Detail of Barbara's drawings and felt frames.

An adornment sure to startle and amuse—a ceremonial beard cover with drawing. Barbara Kensler. Photo courtesy artist.

Decoupage Under Glass Pendants

Decoupage is the art of applying paper cutouts to wood, metal, or other hard surfaces and integrating the cut designs into the background by means of many layers of varnish and a sanded and rubbed finish. Since paper and fabric are not particularly compatible from the standpoint of the paper adhering to the material or enduring washing or cleaning, this would seem a totally useless method of fabric embellishment. Gluing one's designs underneath glass small and lightweight enough to be wearable, and glued to a sturdy fabric backing, is one way to solve this obstacle.

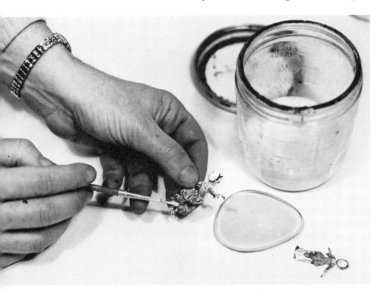

Two figures are cut out with manicure scissors. Glue diluted by one-third with water is brushed on top of the cutouts. The glass pendant that will cover the cutouts is an old eyeglass lens.

The print is pressed against the glass.

A piece of sky blue felt to which bits of fringed green felt have been appliquéd to give the illusion of grass is outlined against the glass in preparation for cutting.

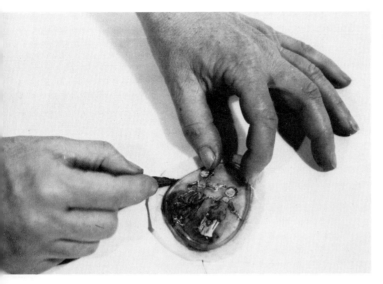

The lens, with its decoupage-and-felt backing, is glued to a larger backing of leather. Beads strung onto lightweight spool wire are glued around the lens edge, with some feathers added as a final decorative touch. An extra piece of fringed leather and feathers completes the pendant.

Vinylized Fabric

By brushing both sides of a cotton fabric with a mixture of half glue and half water or with acrylic medium, the fabric will become nonfraying and firm enough to cut like paper when dry. Thus, fabrics can be used for decoupage or collage fashions. To adhere vinylized fabric to a background, the surface to be covered should be brushed with the vinylizing medium. The cut fabric is placed into the wet medium and glazed with several coats of the medium, with drying time allowed between each coat.

An intricate print has been cut and adhered to a pair of sandals. Four coats of acrylic gloss medium give an attractive, durable, water- and-scuff-proof finish.

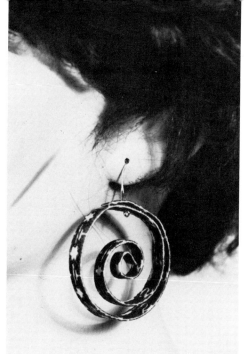

Fabric can be adhered to pieces of cardboard which are then cut, and molded to the desired shape while wet. The gloss medium used to adhere and glaze the armband transforms the soft fabric into a shiny, soft-hard material.

Leftover strips of the fabric-covered cardboard used for the bracelet were coiled into a pair of earrings to match.

Vinylized Flowers

Joanne Ashcraft uses the fabric vinylizing technique somewhat differently to make dainty and very realistic fabric flowers that are equally handsome when worn pinned to a hat, collar, or neckband, or exhibited in a vase. (See Index for other flower pin-on ideas.) Joanne cuts her petals from old sheeting and paints in shading with a small brush, adding the vinylizing mixture only after her flowers are complete.

Two circles of old sheeting were cut into a circle which was in turn shaped into petals. The petals are overlapped into the shape of a rose, then shaped, adhered, and glazed with glue and water. For a very hard glaze, use undiluted glue or acrylic gloss medium.

Daisies—in the making, and finished. The smaller flowers in the jar of roses are violets.

Here is Joanne Ashcraft working at her stencil-painting on fabrics (see Chapter 2), wearing a pretty bunch of fabric daisies.

Latch-Hooked Jewelry

By extending the vinylizing process to canvas, which would ordinarily unravel if cut small and close to the edge, attractive latch-hooked jewelry can be made quickly and easily.

A piece of vinylized canvas bent and twisted to show how firm and intact the edges remain.

The edge or frame of the pendant is covered with single crochet stitches worked into the holes closest to the edge. If not vinylized, this would unravel as the hook is inserted.

The center of a pendant is filled with precut lengths (about two inches each) of rug yarn and a latch hook, available in most yarn supply stores.

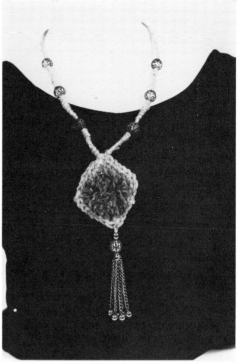

The finished pendants with a wrapped and beaded neckband.

Punch-Hooked Body Adornments

Shirley Lewin is a graphic designer who usually wields her punch hook on large surfaces such as wall hangings and rugs. Occasionally she applies her design and hooking talents to wearable designs.

Shirley Lewin at work with her punch hook.

Man's vest designed and hooked by Shirley Lewin.

Two punch-hooked belts, contoured to conform to the wearer's body.

For those who like the look and texture of punch-hooked rugs but prefer their loops scaled down to smaller adornments, Doreen Sinnett has perfected an interesting tool she calls a minihooker. This needle makes loops the size of small French knots and can be used with any fabric with a slightly open weave.(See Sources of Supplies.)

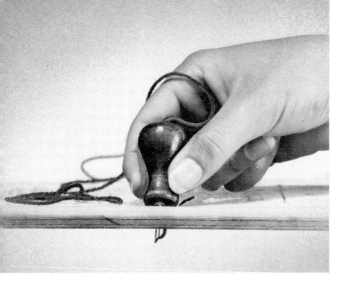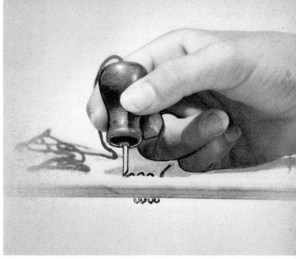

Thread the minihooker (do not put a knot in the yarn) and push the needle all the way through the fabric to be covered. The fabric should have a slightly open weave.

Lift the needle back through the fabric, but keep the point of the needle touching the fabric at all times. *Slide* to the next thread of the fabric (or as close to it as possible) and push the needle all the way through again. Continue like this until a desired color or design area is finished, then snip the yarn close to the fabric and start the next area.

A minihooked pocket by Doreen Sinnett.

Belt embroidered with minihooker rug punch needle by Doreen Sinnett.

A Winding Tool for Yarn Artists

Winding tools to aid in the making of rosettes, pompons, and yarn laces have long fascinated hobbyists.

A winding tool designed for lace making over a hundred years ago, from *Godey's Lady's Book*.

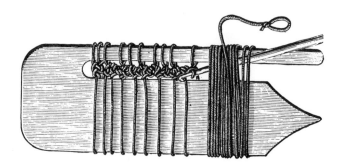

Eleanor Lofton has developed a tool she calls a "hork." It's a simple forklike tool, made in four different sizes ranging from 7 to 10½ inches in length, which in conjunction with a crochet hook can be used to make all sorts of yarn shapes and even a quick-and-easy type of hairpin lace.

The basic idea is to wind yarn around the wider part of the tool and then slide the loops thus made to the smaller part. A small hole at the center is designed for inserting a piece of yarn which will be used to tie the loops. The thickness of the yarn used and the number of turns wound determine the fullness of the shapes made. The addition of crochet stitches determines the final result. The demonstrations and designs that follow are by Eleanor Lofton.

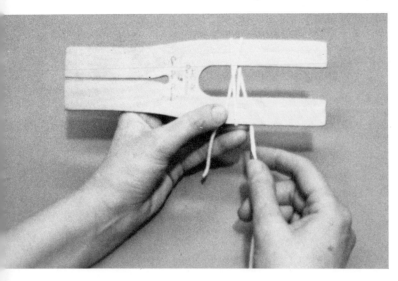

A flower motif is being started on the hork. A 1¼-inch piece of yarn should be left dangling as shown.

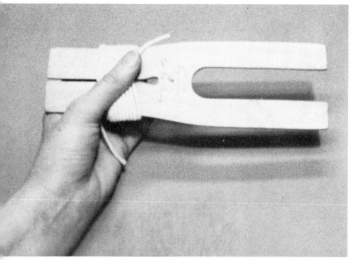

After the desired number of winds are made, the loops are slid to the smaller part of the hork.

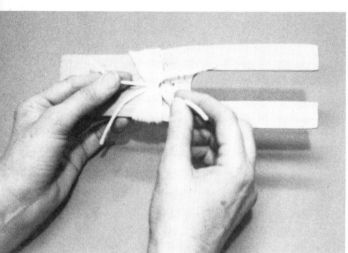

A piece of yarn 6 to 10 inches long is inserted through the hole of the hork and tied around the center of the loops as shown.

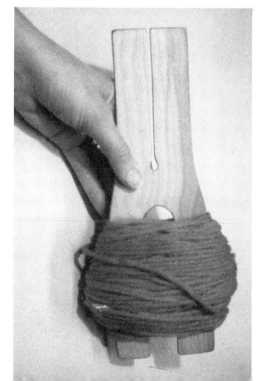

A necklace made of flower motifs made by single crocheting into the outside of each "horked" loop. Readers might compare this with the crocheting methods described in Chapter 6.

For a chrysanthemum fat enough to be used as an earmuff, a large hork is wound three hundred times.

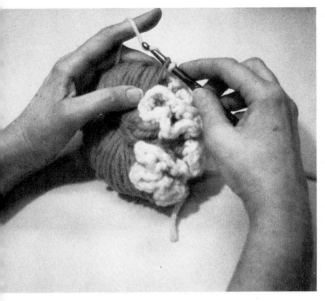

After the center is tied off, each loop is single crocheted for a wavy surface resembling the head of a chrysanthemum.

A chrysanthemum headpiece.

Smaller chrysanthemums can be made by using thinner and fewer yarns. Compare these with the crocheted chrysanthemums on pages 142–43. You may want to try both techniques to see which you like best.

Hairpin Lace Collar

Hairpin lace can be made with Eleanor Lofton's hork or on a wire bent into a U-shaped frame.

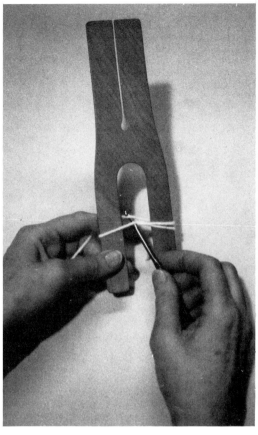

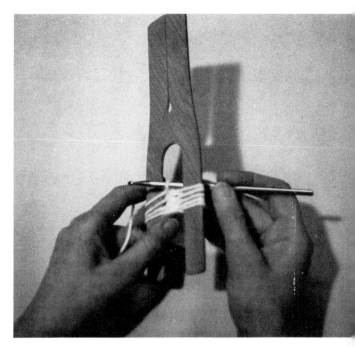

Tie a loop in the center, between the two prongs. Slip a crochet hook under the top strand of the loop and bring the yarn to the back side.

Continue making single crochet stitches down the center.

As the lace becomes longer the finished loops are pulled off.

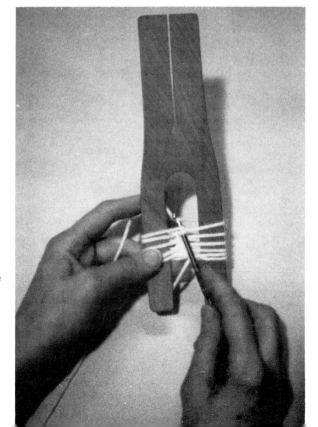

A modern-day version of a sixteenth-century Elizabethan ruff. It's made with poly twine, which allows stiffness without starching. Two lengths of hairpin lace were made on a large hork and sewn on top of one another for fullness.

The collar can also be worn as a Russian-style headpiece.

Stitched and Wired Felt Coils

No discussion of easy-to-use methods and materials would be complete without some new ideas for ways with felt. This versatile fabric's brilliant colors and nonfraying cutting edge make it possible to do things not possible with other fabrics. We've found felt particularly effective when cut into long 1-to-1½''-wide strips which are stitched by machine and then trimmed close to the sewn edge. By inserting wire into the stitched tube, it becomes a flexible coil which can be rolled, twisted, and assembled into all manner of eye-catching and inexpensive jewelry pieces.

A long, one-inch-wide belt strip is machine stitched as close to the folded edge as possible.

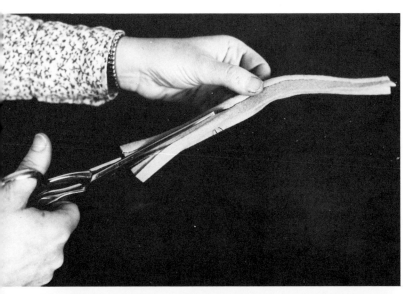

The stitched strip is trimmed right alongside the sewn line.

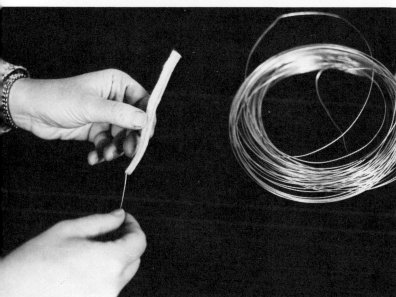

A wire is inserted.

The felt coil can be shaped in many ways.

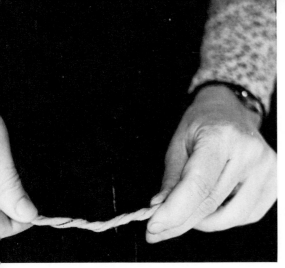

For a different texture, it can be twisted and then coiled.

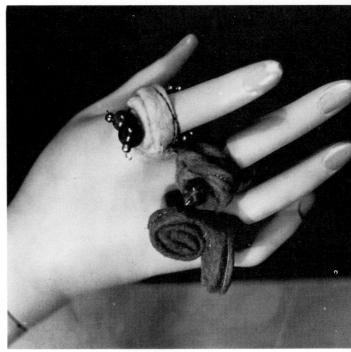

Felt and wire coiled rings.

A completely different kind of felt coil can be made by cutting lots of small, colored felt circles, using a dime as a template.

A holding bead is strung onto monofilament thread and little felt circles are strung into a wiggly coil. Lightweight spool wire could be used as an alternative stringing material.

Dozens of dangle earrings could be made without two ever being alike if color layerings are varied.

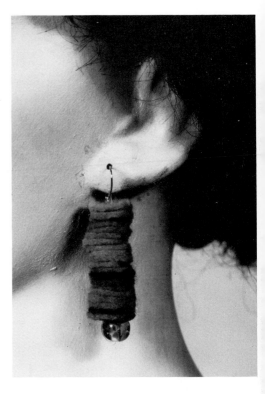

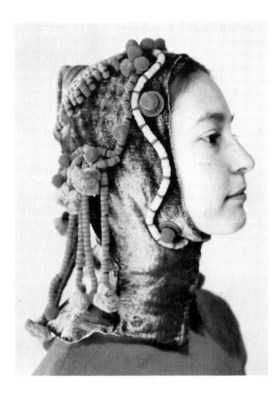

Gayle Stampar appliqués a panne velvet helmet with colorful strung-felt circles. (See color section.)

Yarn and Spool-Wire Braiding

By using a strong but thin fiber like linen or mercerized cotton and braiding it together with lightweight brass wire, a sturdy and very flexible wire-yarn results.

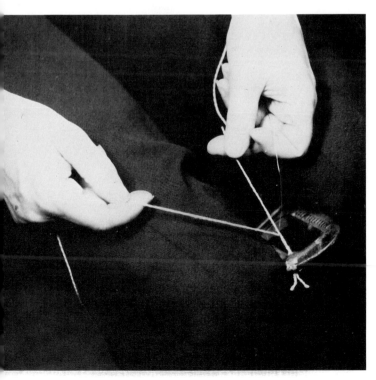

The easiest way to start the braiding is to hold the ends with a small C-clamp and braid with the clamp held between one's knees. To keep the end of the wire-yarn braid from fraying, use a dab of white glue, or a bit of wire, without yarn, twisted into several very tight wraps.

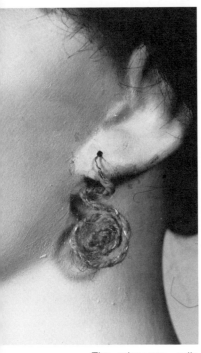
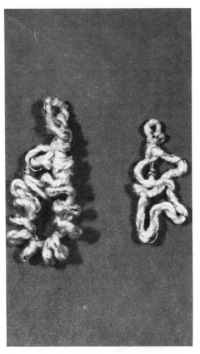
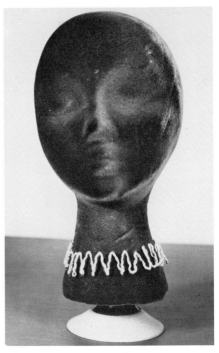

The wire-yarn coils are ideal for making earrings.

Small free-form pendants are also attractive. Note how the top is twisted into a loop which can easily be strung through a neck chain.

This necklace was made by wrapping the wire-yarn around a narrow ruler to produce even twists.

Wire-yarn can serve as a cage for stones and shells. At left a shell is caged, at right a stone. The caging of the painted stone with its unspun wool coiffure is an integral part of the design.

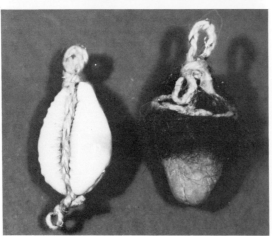

Rear view of caged shell and stone showing the way the wire-yarn is looped and twisted.

No wire is needed to give firmness to heavy cords such as this braided hair ornament with feathers by Jean Boardman Knorr.

Zipper Jewelry

Zippers, though not really fabrics, are such an integral part of sewing that they can indeed be considered a part of the fabric and fiber scene. With old zippers so readily available, those intrigued by the few examples of zipper jewelry shown should have no problem getting hold of lots of this attractive found material.

A large pair of sewing shears and a pair of wire clippers are needed to trim the fabric off the zippers and to cut across the teeth.

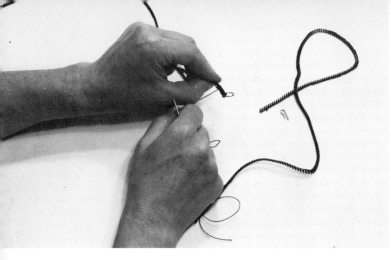

A necklace is being started with two trimmed, brass-colored zippers. A closing hook and ring are wound into the end of the neckband with black button thread.

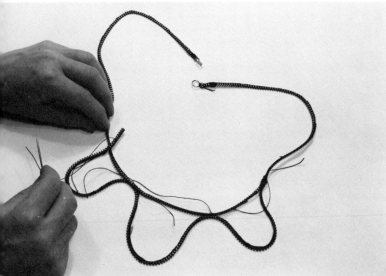

A separate length of zipper is looped onto the neck chain with button thread wrapped down into the teeth of the zipper.

Zippers can be wound into coils and glued to fabric or leather backings. This pendant was made with two lengths of a silver and gold zipper and adhered to leather which is also recycled (an old shoe flap). A green bead is glued to the center of the coil.

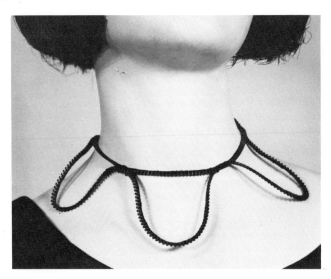

Finished zipper necklace.

10

FUN AND FANTASY

Throughout this book we have tried to strike a balance between body adornments from the workaday world and those which could move to the more special celebrations and events in people's lives. Since celebrations are fitting conclusions to happy experiences, we'd like to conclude with a group of designs which are *all* fun, *all* fantasy. These are celebrations—of the sense of humor, of the love of movement, and of the spirit of fantasy that are happily a part of most people's basic makeup.

Fantasy Ties

When a soft sculptor with Susan Morrison's wit and talent turns her attention to that most ordinary of man's costume accessories, the tie, the results are bound to be splendid and extraordinary. The artist creates a whole series of stocking doll ties as part of a series of American Things. She meticulously dresses her dolls with braids, ribbons, sequins, or whatever else seems appropriate to her statement. (Photographs, Ted Cook.)

Susan dresses her dolls with braids, ribbons, sequins or whatever else seems appropriate to her statement.

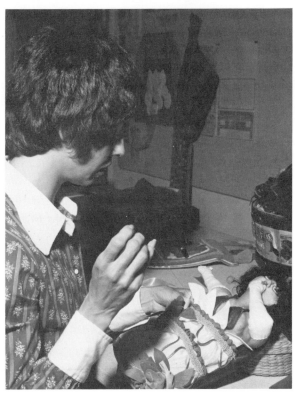

Happy Birthday tie, resplendent with stuffed nylon stocking doll appliqué.

Features are stitched to bring out personality.

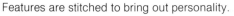

To give the right amount of blush and detail, the dolls are finished off with a brushing of powder and paint.

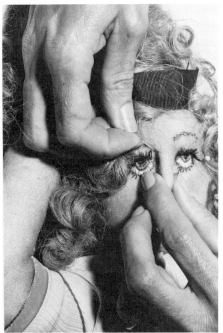

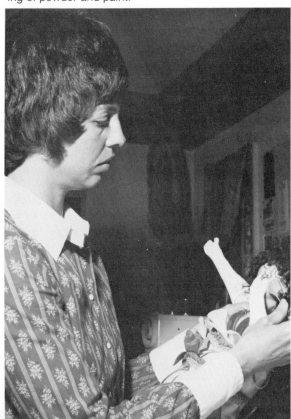

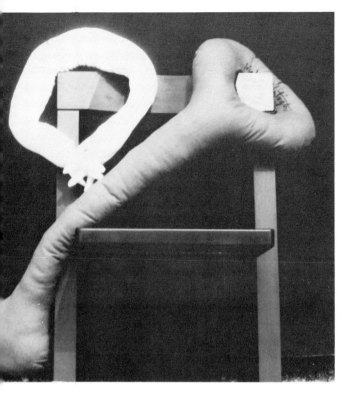

Madge Huntington used sailcloth and stuffing to create two separate interlocking pieces suggestive of limbs and body. The limb loop came first. However, as soon as the arms and hands were finished and crossed, as in the everyday act of crossing one's arms, it became clear that . . .

Body Ornament "Happening"

At times, a piece not really conceived as a body ornament suggests wearability in the course of its development. The almost accidental nature of such a piece might even continue in terms of the wearers use of and play with the design.

. . . loop and arms belong together . . .

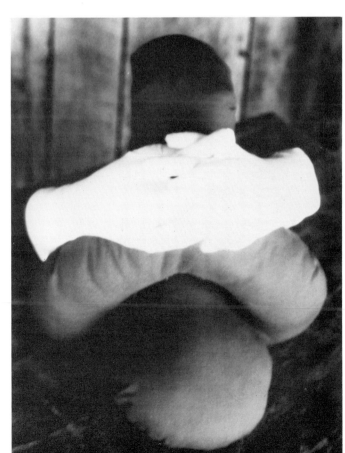

. . . Except when the arms are locked around the artist's neck, much like an old-style fur boa.

Finger Fun

Fingers seem to inspire humor. Here are three artists' clever digital designs.

Sometimes it takes no longer to execute than to think up a fanciful conversation piece like Joan Schulze's St. Patrick's Day Emerald. Fat yarn was stitched into a ring base found in a hobby shop, using knotless netting.

When is a glove not just a glove? The answer, of course, is when it is crocheted, knotless netted, and wrapped by Maggie Brosnan, using "thrums" and residue yarns. Photo courtesy artist.

Maggie's hand adornment has a lovable pet-like personality.

It is also a spirited partygoer.

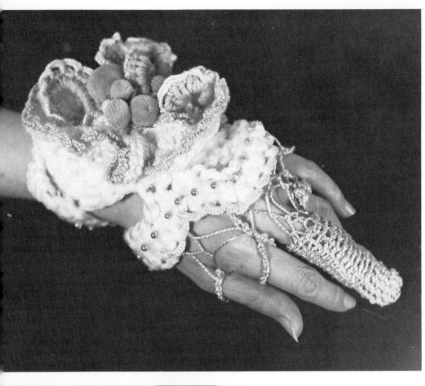

Nancy Lipe's crocheted wrist-and-finger adorn-ment is reminiscent of an Indian slave bracelet.

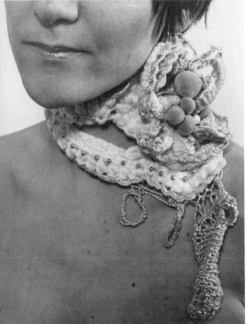

It can do double-duty as a fanciful neckpiece.

To give the piece a proper resting place, Nancy crocheted a small jewelry box.

When finger adornment and box are joined, an ornamental table sculpture is born.

Fantasy Clothes for the Young —and the Young in Heart

By his own admission, it took Picasso thirty-five years to learn to paint once again like a child of six. So many facets of our lives would be brightened if we could hold onto the fun, the wonder, and the innocence of childhood. Sara Wolf-Soley hasn't forgotten the joy of discovering hidden surprises and playacting even as she perfects her skills as a designer-craftsperson. Thanks to Sara's scrupulous attention to every detail of her magical costumes, the results are so fine that they are totally adaptable for use and enjoyment by imaginative and discriminating adults. Fabrics are chosen for accuracy; buttons, inner labels, and linings are treated with utmost respect. More and more, the artist's designs are transcending the category of "for children only."

Spontaneous and fun clothes do not forestall planning and meticulous workmanship, as is obvious from this picture of Sara Wolf-Soley and her assistant, Sally McCann, at work.

This elephant suit features a head which can be buttoned to the bib front or worn as a mask. It is sewn in an amazingly elephantlike fabric, lined with an elephant print, with elephant-motif buttons and a tiny inside pocket; shaped, of course, like an elephant.

Baltimore sculptor Jane Kelly Morais wanted her own "grown-up" elephant suit. Here she is in a splendid all-white version.

For big girls the demure old-fashioned dress becomes a slick and slinky halter top.

Actual gloves are used for the keyboard of this piano dress. The basic dress was adapted from an old pattern.

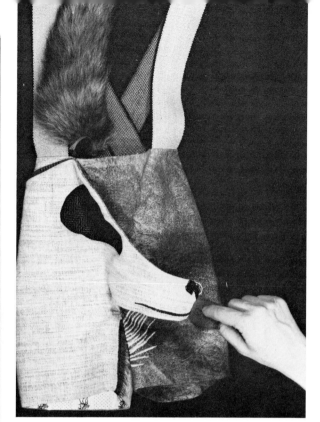

A pair of Hound and Fox pants for a little boy are once again full of Sara's playful surprises: When the fox is unbuttoned from one side to the other . . .

. . . he becomes a wolf. A real fur tail can be pulled out and played with. The lining is also appropriately thematic.

For grown-up boys, the fox and hound theme is transformed into a vest. The fabrics are subdued and sophisticated, the workmanship immaculate, defying any suggestion of cuteness. (See color section.)

A rear view of the vest reveals more surprises: The horse's ears can be tucked in demurely or pulled out during a party. The horse's hair is real horsehair, the fabric is carefully chosen and very organic.

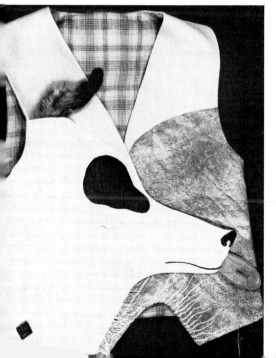

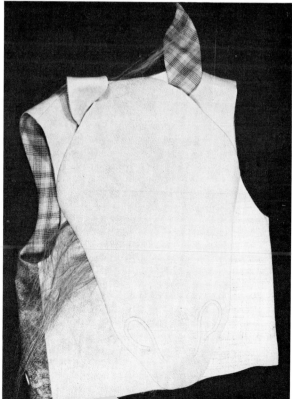

To prove once again that a sense of fun is more important than youth for the enjoyment of fantasy clothes, we photographed this Lettuce and Tomato dress as a tunic top for an adult. The sandwich pocket holds three tomato bags, each to be folded inside the other.

Like all of Sara Wolf-Soley's designs, this Hippo body bag is full of surprises . . .

. . . like the button-off bag and a pull-out-tongue pouch.

Orangutan body bag, an authentic mix of dark brown suede, blue and orange velvet, and silky orange fur.

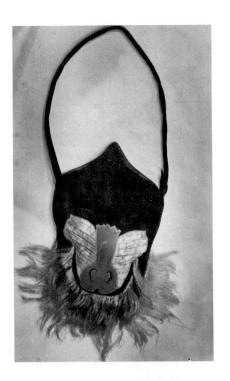

Hats have long intrigued actors as playacting props. This bonnet is for a modern-day Little Red Riding Hood.

It becomes the wicked wolf like this . . .

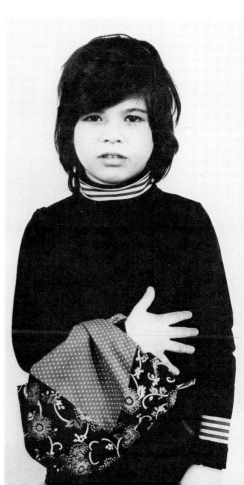

. . . or like this . . .

. . . and, going back to Little Red, here's the hat twisted into a Biscuit Bag for visiting grandma.

MORE HEAD FANTASIES

Eventually, most fiber and fabric artists do a fanciful headpiece. Following are some of our favorites.

The Little Red Riding Hood saga inspired still another fiber fantasy, this one worn by Joellen Sommer for Senior Hat Day, crocheted by Elyse Sommer, and now resting on a terra-cotta head by Mike Sommer. The wolf's head, which is stuffed, started with a tube for the neck. The mouth was made by crocheting two tubes coming out of the head, each stuffed. The teeth are picot stitches. A third, unstuffed, tube was added for the wolf's tongue. The blond curls were made with escalating increases, back and forth along basic crochet chains.

Another crocheted hat fantasy, this one by Nancy Lipe. The artist found the hat esthetically satisfying but not entirely comfortable physically, so she worked it over a wig form, filling out the cheeks with cotton and then permanently gluing the form to an inverted wooden-bowl base. Photo, Dewey Lipe.

Susanna Kuo's batik techniques are detailed in Chapter 2. Here is another example of impeccable workmanship coupled with a fantastic and free-spirited design. The fish helmet is cotton with organdy fins and spines of plastic boning.

Rear view of fish helmet.

Susanna's original sketch plans for the helmet . . .

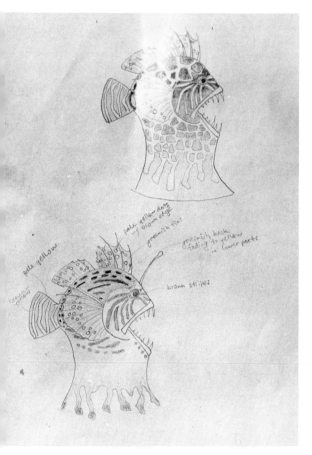

. . . and the pattern pieces which are placed underneath the fabric during wax application.

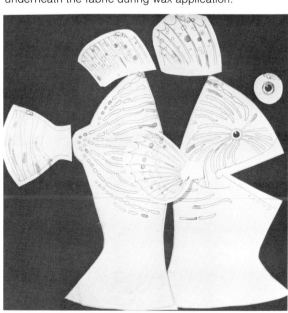

Francie Allen's Tantric Headdress started with a wadded-up ball of string around which she knotted the cupola shape. The rest of the form is built up with wrapping and basketry techniques. Photo, Roger Rosenblatt.

A rear view of the Tantric Headdress.

This rather eerie head-piece is once again built up with coils like a basket. However, this time Francie Allen used actual clay coils for her base. Slits and holes were made into the clay before firing, and an inner lining of batik-dyed burlap was glued to the ceramic shell. Stuffed burlap arrows were sewn to the lining and a stuffed burlap visor was attached with string through a row of holes made at the bottom of the clay shell. Like the real medieval helmets which inspired this one, it is basically too heavy to be considered truly wearable. Photo, Roger Rosenblatt.

223

Hand-built
porcelain
helmet
with
slits
and
holes.

"medieval
battle
helmet"
fired in
kiln to cone 8.

Inner lining
dyed burlap,
glued into
ceramic
shell.

Stuffed
burlap
arrows
protrude
through slits
in ceramic
and sewn to
lining inside.

Stuffed burlap
visor attached with
strings to helmet (see
row of holes at bottom
of clay shell).

Francie Allen's sketches detailing the construction for her medieval helmet.

Here is Barbara Setsu Pickett with a mysterious and magical ceremonial dance shield. Photo, Oscar Palmquist.

Barbara Setsu Pickett's wrapped helmet and vest evoke an almost mystical response in the viewer. Photo, Oscar Palmquist.

A different mood, a different type of dance. The designer is once again Barbara Setsu Pickett. These floating costumes are part of a series of six created for A Dance for Five Tents and a Brick. Photo, Michael Lloyd.

DESIGNED FOR AND BY DREAMERS

Gayle Feller designed her Bird-in-the-Hand Walking-Sleeping Bag for people who fall a-sleep on the couch at night while trying to read or watch television. The bag is worn without garments beneath and fastens at the bottom with Velcro. Hand-dyed velvets, silks, and batiks make the whole thing heaven to wear.

The pillow attached to the sleeping bag has a sleeping face when up. (See color section.)

It is a wide-awake face when down.

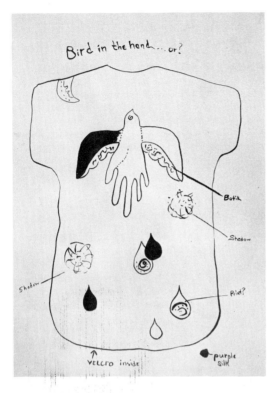

Preliminary sketches for the front of the sleeping bag . . .

. . . and for the rear.

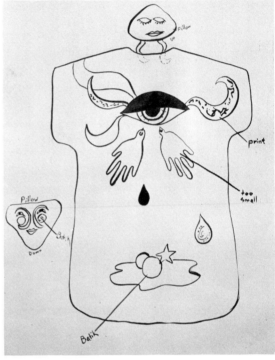

Helen Webster's Great White Bird is a sewn, crocheted, and netted interpretation of a vivid escape dream in which the artist disguised herself as "an inconspicuous great white bird" and perched unobtrusively on lampposts, and so on. Photos courtesy artist.

The flight-deck helmet is exactly what Helen saw in the dream, and found in a surplus store. Needlepoint lace and ostrich feathers were added later.

Quilting detail of Great White Bird wing.

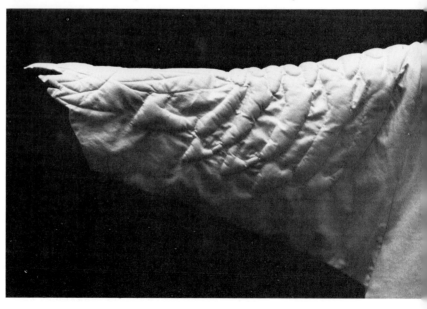

Visionary Techniques for Visionary Designs

Francie Allen began her work as a sculptor in cloth and fiber because of her love for the soft, pliable, and droopy quality of fabric. Some examples of her work were shown earlier. She branched out from fibers into clay. Although she effected some unusual clay and fiber combinations (e.g., the medieval hat, page 222), she felt that the clay-and-fiber involvement pulled her in different directions.

Francie has now begun to make sculptures out of latex rubber which, though neither clay nor cloth, offers the qualities of both. She still uses fibers, frequently incorporating string, raw sisal, and cheesecloth into her latex constructions. For those concerned with working in media that can guarantee some measure of permanency, Francie cautions that latex will begin to deteriorate after a number of years. Since Francie is intensely involved with changes through time and the process of the human mind, this very perishability and impermanence is a quality she seeks for her particular statements.

The medium does allow for experimentation with color as well as form. Francie has added color by mixing the liquid latex with water-based pigment, by painting color into the wet plaster molds before pouring the latex, and by painting on top of the latex after it is poured. (Photographs, Roger Rosenblatt.)

Latex comes in a creamy liquid state and cures on contact with air. Francie Allen buys it in large quantities and transfers it to smaller containers to facilitate handling.

Latex is brushed into a mold made to produce long, flexible tubes. The molds are shaped in clay and cast in plaster.

This was the first time Francie had made a casting of this particular mold, and the casting was not good. It had lots of holes all up and down one side. With true crafts ingenuity the artist utilized her mistake by folding bunches of white cotton string in half and sticking them into the holes. These strings were immediately secured by "gluing" them in with more latex.

Although the latex cures on contact with air, it takes several coats to build up a thick enough layer. Here is the finished form being lifted out of the mold.

It is firm yet pliable.

Francie's latex "boas" have been used by dancers in improvisational workshops and as parts of costumes. (See color section.)

This Rain Dance Cape was made in four parts, each poured in the same basic plaster mold. The separate parts were draped and sewn together to form a cape which also functions as a wall hanging. To create a mottled texture, the finished piece was painted with earth green and rusty purple water-based paints. Holding the piece under running water caused the paint to run and drip, giving a finish reminiscent of something primitive which has just been dug out of the ground.

In Celebration of Weddings

For a bride entering into one of life's major collaborative ventures, this fantastic wedding costume may portend a happy omen, since its design and execution are the result of a highly successful working collaboration between Yvonne Porcella and Maggie Brosnan. (Photographs, Yvonne Porcella.)

The bride wears a tie-dyed silk neckpiece and carries a handpiece made from an abalone shell, encased in knotless netting with found objects and wrapping. Maggie Brosnan and Yvonne Porcella. Photos, Yvonne Porcella.

Rear view of the tie-dyed silk neckpiece for the bride, showing stitched, knotless netted, and wrapped additions.

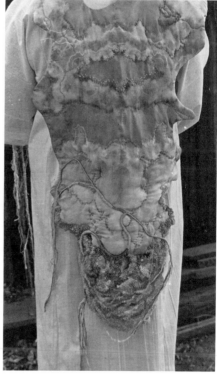

Close-up view of the handpiece. The inside of the shell is pink, with baby's breath.

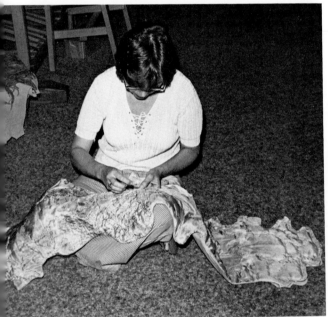

Yvonne worked on the silk neckpiece.

Maggie worked on the handpiece.

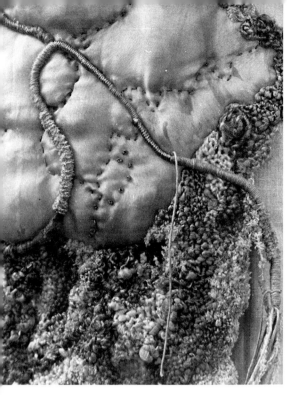

Close-up detail of the knotless netting, stitchery, and wrapping of the neckpiece.

Something Old: Japanese Tin Whistles

Something New: Neckpiece for a Bride

This neckpiece for a bride was designed and stitched by Marilyn Green from white satins and velvet. The fish dangles are Japanese whistles. The satin piece can be removed from the frog closing for cleaning. The neckband is a drapery cord.

Bibliography

Alexander, Marthann. *Simple Weaving*. New York: Taplinger, 1969.

Allen, Elsie. *Pomo Basketmaking*. Healdsburg, Calif.: Naturegraph Publishers, 1972.

Ashley, Clifford W. *The Ashley Book of Knots*. New York: Doubleday, 1944.

Birrell, Vera. *The Textile Arts*. New York: Harper & Brothers, 1959.

Caulfield, Sophie Frances Anne, and Seward, Blanche C. *The Dictionary of Needlepoint*. Facsimile editions. New York: Arno Press and Dover, 1972.

Christopher, Frederick John. *Basketry*. New York: Dover, 1952.

Dawson, Mary. *A Complete Guide to Crochet Stitches*. New York: Crown, 1972.

De Dillemont, Therese. *Encyclopedia of Needlework*. Milhouse, France. Facsimile edition. Philadelphia: Running Press, 1972.

Dean, Beryl. *Creative Appliqués*. New York: Watson-Guptill, 1970.

Dendel, Esther Warner. *Needleweaving . . . Easy as Embroidery*. New York: Doubleday,1972.

Ellsworth, Evelyn Peters. *Textiles and Costume Design*. San Francisco: Paul Elder, 1917.

Harvey, Virginia I. *Macramé: The Art of Creative Knotting*. New York: Van Nostrand Reinhold, 1963.

Hemmand, Larry. *Leathercraft*. New York: Doubleday, 1972.

Johnson, Meda Parker, and Kaufman, Glen. *Design on Fabric*. New York: Van Nostrand Reinhold, 1967.

Kafka, Francis J. *The Hand Decoration of Fabrics*. New York: Dover, 1959.

Koenig, René. *A La Mode*. New York: Seabury Press, 1971.

Krevitsky, Nik. *Stitchery: Art and Craft*. New York: Van Nostrand Reinhold, 1968.

McKim, Ruby Short. *One Hundred and One Patchwork Patterns*. New York: Dover, 1962.

Meilach, Dona Z. *Contemporary Batik and Tie-Dye*. New York: Crown 1973.

———. *Contemporary Leather*. Chicago: Henry Regnery, 1971.

———. *Macramé: Creative Design in Knotting*. New York: Crown, 1971.

Mon Tricot Knitting Dictionary. New York: Crown, 1972.

Mosley, Spencer; Johnson, Pauline; and Koenig, Hazel. *Craft Design*. Belmont, Calif.: Wadsworth, 1962.

Newman, Thelma. *Leather as Art and Craft*. New York: Crown, 1973.

100 Embroidery Stitches. Book #150. New York: Coats and Clark Co., 1973.

Parker, Xenia Ley. *Working with Leather*. New York: Charles Scribner's, 1972.

Peterson, Grete, and Svennas, Else. *Handbook of Stitches*. New York: Van Nostrand Reinhold, 1970.

Rainey, Sarita R. *Weaving without a Loom*. Worcester, Mass.: Davis, 1969.

Roach, Mary Ellen, and Bubolz Eicher, Joanne. *Dress Adornment and the Social Order*. New York: John Wiley, 1965.

Rome, Carol Cheney, and Devlin, Georgia French. *A New Look at Needlepoint*. New York: Crown, 1972.

Sommer, Elyse. *Contemporary Costume Jewelry: A Multimedia Approach*, New York: Crown, 1974.

———. *Decoupage Old and New*. New York: Watson-Guptill, 1971.

———, and Sommer, Joellen. *A Patchwork, Appliqué, and Quilting Primer*. New York: Lothrop, Lee, & Shepard, 1975.

———, and Sommer, Mike. *A New Look at Crochet*. New York: Crown, 1975.

———, and Sommer, Mike. *A New Look at Felt: Stitchery, Appliqué, and Sculpture*. New York: Crown, 1975.

Sommer, Joellen, with Sommer, Elyse. *Sew Your Own Accessories*. New York: Lothrop, Lee, & Shepard, 1972. Simon & Schuster, Pocket Books, 1973.

Thomas, Mary. *Mary Thomas's Embroidery Book*. New York: William Morrow, 1936.

Wilson, Jean. *Weaving Is for Anyone*. New York: Van Nostrand Reinhold, 1967.

Wooster, Ann-Sargent. *Quiltmaking*. New York: Drake, 1972.

Publications

The following publications may be of interest as ongoing sources of information about craft developments, shows, and new sources of supplies.

Artweek
Box 2496
Castro Valley, Calif. 94546
Weekly newspaper.

Crafts Horizon
American Craftsmen's Council
44 W. 53rd St.
New York, N.Y. 10019
Bimonthly.

Creative Crafts
Drawer 700
Newton, N.J. 96869
Bimonthly.

Needle Arts
120 E. 56th St.
New York, N.Y. 10022
Quarterly journal of Embroiderer's
    Guild of America, available
    with membership.

Open Chain
632 Bay Road
Menlo, Park, Calif. 94025
Monthly newsletter for textile artists.

Quilter's Newsletter
Box 394
Wheat Ridge,Colo. 80033
Monthly.

Westart
Box 1396
Auburn, Calif. 94546
Semimonthly.

Shuttle, Spindle and Dye Pot
339 Steele Rd.
W. Hartford, Conn. 06111
Quarterly journal of Handweaver's
    Guild, available with member-
    ship.

Sources of Supplies

The materials needed to create soft jewelry and body adornments are readily available from local stores. Many supplies are likely to be found right around the reader's own house.

Fabric and notions stores, as well as stores selling knitting, crochet, and needlework supplies, are located in practically every neighborhood. Check your classified directory for Weavers' Supplies, Cordage Supplies, Marine Supplies, Upholstery Materials, Leather, Beads, Feathers, and Shells. Most areas have an art supplies store or a general paint store which stocks art supplies for painting and printing.

For out-of-the-way materials and bargains, visit garage sales, flea markets, and antique shops. The following listing was compiled to give the reader an opportunity to shop by mail and thus geographically expand his supply sources. It is impossible to make such a listing a definitive one. Omission of any names in no way implies a negative judgment on our part, but simply that we can know about just so many suppliers; nor should inclusion be interpreted as our personal endorsement.

Catalogs are costly to print and mail, so most suppliers charge for this service, though in some instances the cost of the catalog is deductible from the first order. Where no charge is listed, it can be assumed that price lists, catalogs, or samples are free. However, to ensure prompt replies, it is always advisable to include a stamped, self-addressed envelope—letter-sized if you want a price sheet, manila-sized if a catalog or samples are requested.

Beads, Leather, Jewelry Findings

Check under "Fibers and Dyes" below for additional sources.

Bead Game
505 N. Fairfax Ave.
Los Angeles, Calif. 90336
Beads, mirrors, leathers, and
    suedes. Catalog 50¢.

Berman's
147 South St.
Boston, Mass. 02109
Leather.

Cooper Mountain Trading Co.
7645 Miller Hill Rd.
Aloha, Ore. 97005
Puka shells, all sizes. Samples, $3.

Derby Lane Shell Center
10515 Gandy Blvd.
St. Petersburg, Fla. 33702
Shells and findings. Catalog $1.

Earthy Endeavors
Box 817
Whittier, Calif. 90608
Ceramic beads, glazed and un-
    glazed.

Indiana Leather Supply Co.
216 S. Indiana
Bloomington, Ind. 47401

Jasmine and Bead
207 Fairfield Pike
Yellow Springs, Ohio 45387
Imported beads.

Jewelart
7753 Densmore Ave.
Van Nuys, Calif. 90027
Findings, chains, beads. Catalog
    $1.

Leathercraft Supplies
25 Great Jones St.
New York, N.Y. 10012

Riverstone Crafts
1654 N. Cleveland
Chicago, Ill. 60614
Ceramic and metal beads. Catalog
    $1.

Sax Arts and Crafts
207 N. Milwaukee
Milwaukee, Wisc. 53202
Leathers.

Sheru
49 W. 38th St.
New York, N.Y. 10018
Specializes in beads; also yarns,
    metal cords, findings.

Sy Schweitzer & Co.
Box 431
E. Greenwich, R.I. 02818
Chains, findings. Catalog 50¢.

Tandy Leathers
See local classified directory.

Walbead
8 W. 37th St.
New York, N.Y. 10018
Beads, mirrors.

Lee Ward
840 N. State St.
Elgin, Ill. 60120
Beads, leathers, general supplies.

Fibers and Dyes

C. M. Almy & Sons, Inc.
37 Purchase St.
Rye, N.Y. 10021
Metal threads.

Berga/Ullman
Box 831 L
Westerly Rd.
Ossining, N.Y. 10562
Swedish wool. Samples $3. Very prompt shipments.

Dick Blick
Box 1268
Galesburg, Ill. 61401
They have a special weavers' catalog and a general arts and crafts supplies catalog; a comprehensive source.

William Condon & Sons
65 Queen St.
Charlottetown, P.E.I., Canada

Contessa Yarns
Box 37
Lebanon, Conn. 06247
Novelty yarns. News announcements to customers.

Coulter Studios
118 E. 59th St.
New York, N.Y. 10022
Imported and domestic yarns, weaving equipment, dyes, books.

Countryside Handweavers
Box 1225
Mission, Kans. 66222

Craft Gallery
96 S. Broadway
South Nyack, N.Y. 10060
Metal threads.

Crafts Kaleidoscope
6551 Ferguson St.
Indianapolis, Md. 46220
Cords, yarns, beads, and books.

Crafts Yarns of Rhode Island
Box 385
Pawtucket, R.I. 02862
Yarns, cords, novelties. Samples 50¢.

Dharma Trading Co.
Box 1288
Berkeley, Calif. 94701
Yarns, cords, dyes. Samples 50¢.

Frederick Fawcett, Inc.
129 South St.
Boston, Mass. 02111
Linens. Samples $1.

Fiber Studio
Box 356
Sudbury, Mass. 01776
Rug yarns, novelties.

Folklorico
Box 625
Palo Alto, Calif. 94302

Fort Crailo Yarns Co.
2 Green St.
Rensselaer, N.Y. 12144
Wools, cottons.

Freed & Co.
Box 394
Albuquerque, N. Mex. 87101
Yarns, beads, shells, leathers.

Greentree Ranch Wools
163 N. Carter Lake Rd.
Loveland, Colo. 80537
Imported and domestic yarns, raw fleece, dyes, weaving equipment.

Louise Groose Ltd.
36 Manchester St.
London, W.1, England
Silks, braids, metal threads.

Handcrafts from Europe
Box 372
Sausalito, Calif. 94965
Metal threads.

P. C. Herwig Co., Inc.
R. 2, Box 140
Milaca, Minn. 56353
Yarn, beads, stuffing. Catalog
    50¢.

Lamb's End
165 W. 9 Mile Rd.
Ferndale, Mich. 48220
Fibers, feathers, beads, shells,
    stuffing materials. Samples
    $1.

Lily Mills
Shelby, N.C. 28150
Catalog $1.

The Mannings
East Berlin, Pa. 17316
All types of yarns, cords, equip-
    ment, beads, and books.
    Catalog 50¢.

Naturalcraft
2199 Bancroft Way
Berkeley, Calif. 94704
Yarns, cords, beads, shells, and
    feathers. Catalog 50¢.

Pendleton Shop
Box 233
Sedona, Ariz. 86336
Yarns, buttons, beads, mounting
    rings.

Potomac Yarns
Box 2368
Chapel Hill, N.C. 27514
Inexpensive earth-colored acryl-
    ics. Free samples.

Screen Process Supplies
1199 E. 12th St.
Oakland, Calif. 94606
Inko dyes and other batik ma-
    terials.

Straw Into Gold
Box 2904
Oakland, Calif. 94618
Yarns, beads, books; very read-
    able catalog, 75¢

Tahki Imports
336 West End Avenue
New York, N.Y. 10023
Imported yarns, stuffing.

Toye, Kennington and Spencer
    Ltd.
Regalia St., Red Lion Square
London, W.C. 1, England
Metal threads.

Tuxedo Yarn and Needlepoint
36-35 Main Street
Flushing, N.Y. 11354
Yarns, beads, and stuffing.

Yarn Depot, Inc.
545 Sutter St.
San Francisco, Calif. 94102
Yarns, beads, books.

Yarn Primitives
Box 1013
Weston, Conn. 06880
Imported yarns, Samples
    $2.

Miscellaneous

Adhesive Products
1660 Boone Avenue
Bronx, N.Y. 10460
Liquid latex.

Ashcrafts
P. O. Box 1411
Greenwood, Miss. 38930
Fabric-painting design books.

Binney & Smith
380 Madison Avenue
New York, N.Y. 10017
Crayola fabric crayons.

Durable Arts
Box 2413
San Rafael, Calif. 94901
Versatex textile paints.

General Latex and Chemical Corp.
Box 498
Ashland, Ohio 44805
Liquid latex.

HobbyCraft, Inc.
Box 40
Monmouth, Ill. 61464
Liquid latex, general crafts.

Home-Sew, Inc.
1825 W. Market St.
Bethlehem, Pa. 18018
Free twenty-page illustrated cata-
    log of laces, ribbons, zippers,
    Velcro, and other sewing-
    supply specialties.

Screen Process Supplies
1199 E. 12th St.
Oakland, Calif. 94606
Photosensitive dyes.

Sinnett Designs
418 Santa Ana Avenue
Newport Beach, Calif. 92660
Minihookers.

Studio Workshop
6708 N. E. Roselawn
Portland, Ore. 97218
Hork tool.

3M Color Center
845 Third Avenure
New York, N.Y. 10017
Write for address of color center
    near you.

Index